Whole Body Fitness

WHOLE BODY

Training Mind, Body, and Spirit

WHOLE BODY FITNESS
Training Mind, Body, and Spirit

BY DAN MILLMAN

How to master yourself—and your life—through physical training

Building on fifteen years of experience in every phase of athletics, supplemented by studies in kinesthetics, nutrition, psychology and the martial arts and movement yogas of the Orient, Dan Millman presents a practical and inspirational guide to complete fitness which can help everybody from the professional athlete to the Sunday jogger. Because of his wide-ranging professional experience in Western sports and his intensive studies in the techniques of the East, highlighted by a year spent traveling around the world and learning aikido, karate, t'ai chi, and various yogas from the masters, Millman knows how to combine the wisdom and practical training of East and West to map out a path for physical, mental, and emotional development which can lead to greater control of every aspect of our daily lives.

A commonsensical, reassuring step-by-step guide, *Whole Body Fitness* is packed with specific suggestions, aphoristic insights, anecdotes and examples, plus a healthy dose of old-fashioned inspiration. Dozens of exercises, both physical and metal, teach you how to move your body, and show you how the mind and emotions affect it. Unlike the usual touch-your-toes and run-in-place-for-five-minutes routine, these exercises are exercises in self-discovery. After performing, you will never again think of body, mind, and emotions as mutually exclusive, and you will see how an understanding of their interdependence can help you reduce stress and increase energy.

Dan Millman's whole body approach to athletics applies as much to life as to sports, and should benefit athletes at all levels, as well as dancers, martial artists, yoga students, and the millions of people who are rediscovering the benefits of physical activity in daily life. *Whole Body Fitness* will help you move with spirit along all the paths of life.

DAN MILLMAN was born in Los Angeles, received his B.A. from the University of California at Berkeley, and is a world champion gymnast. He has taught gymnastics, acrobatics, and movement to men and women at Stanford University, Oberlin College, and Berkeley. Oberlin gave him a one-year grant to travel and study in the East, enabling him to combine the disciplines of East and West in his teaching, and aiding him in his own athletic pursuits, which range from archery to yoga, from badminton to trampoline, from white water rafting to ballet. At present, he resides in Oberlin, Ohio, with his wife, Joy, who appears on the jacket photo along with her husband.

FITNESS

DAN MILLMAN

Clarkson N. Potter, Inc./Publishers NEW YORK
DISTRIBUTED BY CROWN PUBLISHERS, INC.

12/94

Inquiries should be addressed to Clarkson N. Potter, Inc.,
One Park Avenue, New York, N.Y. 10016

Printed in the United States of America

Published simultaneously in Canada by General
Publishing Company Limited

Library of Congress Cataloging in Publication Data

Millman, Dan.
  Whole Body Fitness.
  1. Athletics—Psychological aspects. I. Title.
GV706.4.M54 1979   796′.01   79-14619
ISBN 0-517-53852-0

*To my dad, who was my first athletic idol, and to
my mom, who loved me even when I fell on my face*

Contents

Preface

Nearly every household in America has a TV set, a couch, hot-and-cold running water . . . and a couple of aspiring athletes to put them to appropriate use. The TV set may be tuned to *Wide World of Sports*; the couch is supporting big brother's back after his squash game; the hot-and-cold water is soaking Sissy's gymnastics leotard. Mom and Dad, who were once fierce bridge players, are now the terrors of the tennis court. Cousin Bessy has just started jogging, and Uncle Irv lives on the golf course.

All over America, people are emulating the star athletes. The stars themselves are still striving upward. Our entire culture is slipping into something more comfortable and going out to run. The space age is only a minor attraction. This is the Age of the Athlete.

Today's magazines are filled with articles on how athletics are good for you. Sports seem to be the ultimate remedy for everything from a sluggish sex life to the variety of psychological woes endemic to our society. Athletes are slimmer, stronger, more attractive. They possess greater energy, confidence, and assertiveness. One of our culture's most admired archetypes is the happy, friendly, and intelligent athlete. It seems such *fun* to be an athlete. If only it were a little easier to become one.

We all like to learn well, fast, and easily—whether we're preparing for a Sunday jog or the Olympic decathlon. But with very few exceptions, the training process is a difficult encounter, laden with obstacles, frustrations, and often pain. Even the pros and the Olympians have their peaks and depressions. We all envy the *natural athlete,* who apparently was born to excel without struggling.

What we fail to recognize is that Mom, Dad, and Cousin Bessy were all natural athletes in their infancy, before their minds became clouded with self-consciousness, fear of failure, and self-judgment, before their bodies grew stiff with tension. Everyone begins life with nearly unlimited human potential.

Though most of us have lost touch with our childhood aptitudes, we still slog onward toward our dreams and aspirations, through virtually unmapped territory, choosing teachers and taking advice at random, trying valiantly to "follow through, turn the wrist under, stay aggressive, keep the eye on the ball, hold the hips counterrotational, move faster . . ." and so it goes.

This book attempts to map out a systematic approach to reclaiming your original potential in the gym, on the field, and throughout daily life. It outlines a natural process of training which incorporates the conscious development and integration of body, mind, and emotions.

First, in "Understanding the Game," you'll learn to observe the lessons of nature, use the power of awareness, and realign yourself with the natural laws.

In "Developing Talent," you'll see how physical, mental, and emotional talent can be developed.

"Moving with Spirit" clarifies the techniques of natural training, and includes insight into the benefits and liabilities of the competitive experience. This section ends with a vision of the evolution of sport and the games of tomorrow.

The final section, "Achieving Unity," approaches overall human development through athletic training from an Eastern perspective—beginning with the training of the master athlete and ending with insight into sport, meditation, and the spiritual experience.

NOTE TO THE READER

The word "athlete" is a romantic, universal symbol. It usually refers to someone who explores the limits of his capacity, especially (though not exclusively) through strength, stamina, speed or agility in sports or games. The process of *training*, rehearsing, or practicing in order to improve is a central concern of every athlete.

Even the weekend athlete is always training to improve his game. Dancers, jugglers, musicians, mimes, martial artists, and every kind of movement performer are equally involved in the process of training. Therefore, I include them all in the realm of athletics. It is these athletes in every walk of life for whom this book was written.

We perceive and relate to the world from three centers in the human body: the *head* (intellect); the *heart* (emotions); and the *belly* (movement vitality). The intellectual center deals with *understanding*, the emotional center with *energy*, the movement center with *action*. Since we want to keep the three in balance and cultivate each of them, it is essential to give each equal attention in a complete system of training.

Becoming a total athlete is a process which involves reawakening the full capacity of all three centers. The intellect is the map, the emotions are the fuel, and movement is the vehicle of training. The secret to success lies in balancing and harmonizing the three centers.

Books are generally subject to the literary limitation of reaching only two centers. They offer information (head) and inspiration (heart). In order to offer a whole-body experience, I've added various exercises in boxed sections throughout the book so you can do and feel what the words say. Physically doing the exercises can increase the book's value to you, many times over.

Consider this quote, attributed to an anonymous Chinese sage:

I hear and I forget.
I see and I remember.
I do and I understand.

In closing, I should note that becoming a natural athlete is equally possible for men and women. However, I have chosen to use the terms "he," "his," and "man" in place of the awkward "he-or-she," "his-or-hers," etc. The use of masculine nominatives is a literary device only. As a women's gymnastics coach, I have had ample opportunity to appreciate the awesome beauty, grace, and dynamic abilities of the female athlete.

INTRODUCTION
The natural athlete in action

The announcer's voice quivers with excitement as the film flickers on the screen: "Ladies and gentlemen, you are about to see a feat performed for the first time by David Seale—a feat requiring the full extension of his concentration, daring, and coordination. What you are about to observe did not happen overnight, but was the result of months of preparation. Here he goes!"

A figure appears on the screen. David looks relaxed and confident, about to begin a complex series of movements and balances. He stands momentarily poised on the brink, hesitates only briefly. Then, with eyes focused ahead, not looking down, his mind apparently paying total attention to the task at hand, he begins to move. His body remains relaxed in the face of this first successful attempt.

As his primary movement continues, there is a sudden tremor . . . and he falls! Quickly, automatically, he catches himself as he has learned to do before. Without wasting a moment on anger or fear, he stands again and continues toward his goal. David's face shows only serenity and concentration.

As he nears the goal he has another near miss, but again

regains his balance. Then he reaches out, his face beaming. After a brief final moment of suspense, those watching the film let out their breath and applaud with delight, as diapered, ten-month-old David Seale, a natural athlete, reaches out and grasps his mother's outstretched arms. Recorded by his father's movie camera, David has walked his first steps, all the way across the living-room rug.

In any nursery we can find the natural athlete in action. Our attention has been so captivated by the Olympian heights that we often forget the extraordinary miniature athletes at our feet. The infant's gift for learning is undeniable. Sensitive observation of children can reveal the keys to their natural aptitudes. We can see that the infant's body is relaxed, therefore sensitive. His mind is concept free, therefore receptive. His uninhibited emotions account for his great motivational energy. The young child learns complex patterns of speech and movement with an ease and rapidity that is astonishing.

You were once that natural athlete. Your potential was practically unlimited in any field of endeavor—but then something happened. The socialization process which gave you essential information also inflicted upon you fears, associations, beliefs, attitudes, and concepts that drew you out of the natural pattern of infancy. Your mind formed an illusory self-concept; you learned to criticize yourself; you began to fear failure. Emotional constrictions and inhibitions resulted in physical tension. As you grew, you began to struggle with gravity and to develop a variety of psychophysical imbalances and compensations. That's why athletic training—and learning in general—can seem difficult.

This book represents a way to regain your birthright as a natural athlete. By identifying the natural laws which manifest themselves in the world and in your psyche, you can discover once again how to align yourself with these laws. In learning how to learn you can train with ease, improve with certainty, and attain your true potential.

Athletics and the Game of Life

Since we develop ourselves only in response to a demand, it's fair to assume that integrated development of body, mind, and emotions will happen only through an activity that makes such a simultaneous demand on all three centers. Yet in most of our daily experiences, the jobs we practice and interests we pursue require specialized skills and only make demands on isolated portions of our total capacities. For example, some people are involved predominantly in mental or intellectual work; others may develop emotional sensitivity; still others—as in athletics—may refine physical skills.

The training of the natural athlete has maximum carry-over into daily life, because it is always oriented to balanced development of all three centers. Thus, his whole-body development has benefits at the home or in the office, since the mental clarity and emotional stability he refines affects his every endeavor . . . while the benefits of specialized coordination or developed musculature end at the gym.

What most of us look for in athletics are physical exercise, recreation, and a higher level of fitness—with only casual or random attention to developing the mind or emotions. The message which is the motive force behind this book is that *you can gain much more than you might have anticipated.* In order to develop our total capacities for life—the subtle as well as the gross qualities—you have to know precisely what you're looking for.

If a pickpocket stands in a crowd of saints, all he sees are their pockets.

—**anonymous**

To develop your strength, you don't just exercise one arm, ignoring the rest of the body. The natural process of training then, helps create an athlete who is skilled . . . *and* smart . . . *and* serene. Such a man or woman is fully trained for the rigors of daily life as well as those in the gymnasium. In the past, such whole-body training was found only in the Eastern traditions or in more ancient cultures. It is the same educational process advocated by Plato and Socrates who, in fact, often lectured in the gymnasium.

God, I should say, has given men two arts: Music, and gymnastics.
—**Plato**

Influenced by the ancient traditions, our culture is rediscovering a vast array of routes to body-mind harmony. Athletics can incorporate and absorb these systems to create a new breed of athlete. This natural athlete may demonstrate only modest or subtle gains in the arena, but will shine like never before in daily life.

Whether or not you aspire to the peaks of athletic prowess, you can become a natural athlete, and thereby enhance the quality of your daily life. The techniques and insights that progressively unfold in this book will inevitably improve your game. It is my hope that you will apply your athletic game to the Games of Life.

In or out of the gymnasium, proper training always requires energy and commitment. This book outlines a possibility, and shows you a path. The rest is up to you.

D.M.
Berkeley, California
June 1978

Whole Body Fitness

Part One

The Map

Understanding the game

Training—the heart of the athletic experience—can be represented by a journey up a mountain path. Each one of us has been given a different-size mountain to climb during our life. The peak represents our highest potential.

Wherever you now stand on your own mountain—near the base or up in the clouds—it's wise to have a map of the terrain ahead, so you avoid drifting or wandering aimlessly. You need to know precisely where you're headed, and how to get there.

The next few chapters represent this map of understanding, which serves as an aerial photograph, giving you a realistic perspective for the journey. In this way you can see your exact position relative to your goals, get an idea of the obstacles in your path, and gauge the effort that will be required to reach your next goal.

Realistic vision allows you to choose the wisest paths relative to your chosen goals. You may discover that the course which appears shortest may not be the quickest. Understanding this, you can retrace steps if necessary, make course corrections and appropriate preparations, and perhaps even redefine your immediate goals.

The map is your first vital element in a successful journey. Understanding is the proper beginning. It's said that from a good beginning, all things come naturally.

1 THE LESSONS OF NATURE

Rules of the game

For fifteen years I trained with great energy in the sport of gymnastics. In order to succeed (and even survive) I had to develop every conceivable athletic quality, including strength, suppleness, speed of reflexes, stamina, coordination, agility, balance, and a kinesthetic sense, as well as psychological qualities of courage, intense concentration, and serenity.

No matter how hard I applied myself, the process of learning seemed intolerably slow and frustrating. I just couldn't accept the random, haphazard way I learned. Eventually I began to study the process of learning.

Beginning with standard psychological theory, I read every current study of motivation, reinforcement, and learning I could lay my hands on. My understanding grew, but only in bits and pieces. Extensive reading of Eastern philosophy opened up new perspectives, but still the puzzle remained. Then I abandoned experts, theories, and books—and turned to my own intuition.

I remembered the fact that infants learn at a remarkable pace compared to adults. I began then to watch my little daughter at play, to see if I couldn't discover what qualities she possessed that most adults lacked.

Early one Sunday morning I was watching Holly play with the cat on the kitchen floor. My eyes darted from Holly to the cat and back again. Just then, a vision began to crystallize; an intuition was forming about the development of talent—not just physical talent, but emotional and mental talent as well.

I had noticed that Holly's approach to play was as relaxed and mindless as the cat's. I realized that the essence of talent is not so much the *presence* of certain qualities, but rather the *absence* of self and society-imposed obstructions. Young children appear to be free of the mental, physical, and emotional obstructions which we unconsciously develop in our later years.

After that discovery, I decided that if there were any ultimate clues to be found, they would appear in the precivilized world of nature. I found myself taking long walks alone, observing the natural forces and their relationship to the creatures and vegetation and to the earth. At first, I only skimmed the surface, recording the obvious— that plants tend to grow toward the sun, that objects fall toward the earth and rivers flow downhill. These were elementary-school observations; yet I didn't know how else to begin.

After many such walks, my vision cleared. Nature removed her veil, and I was able to see her lessons. I saw trees bending in the wind, and understood the principle of *nonresistance*. Visualizing how gentle running water can cut through solid rock, I grasped the law of *accommodation*. Seeing how all living things thrived in moderate cycles, I was able to understand the principle of *balance*. Observing the regular passing of the seasons, each coming in its own good time, taught me the *natural order* of life.

I realized that I had become alienated from the natural pattern, but that my daughter still knew no separation from *things as they are*. After all my searching, these insights were a delight to me—and gave new meaning to athletic training. Still, it all seemed more poetical than practical . . . until, all in a single moment, the final piece fell into place.

I was taking a warm shower, enjoying the soothing spray. My thoughts were quiet; then out of nowhere, a realization came and left me stunned: "The laws are psychophysical!" This may not seem like a great realization to you, but I dropped the soap.

Realizing that nature's laws applied equally to the human psyche, inseparable from the human body, made all the difference for me. With that the world turned upside-down. No longer would I view the principles of my training as merely physical in their implications. From that day on, athletic training was to become a *psycho*physical challenge. The world no longer seemed just a static physical object. Now it was filled with energy and movement and subtle things. This episode reconnected my psyche to the universal laws, and reaffirmed my essential participation in nature.

All that remained was to put this understanding to use—to apply it fully to a new way of athletic training. Through such training we could all reawaken our innate ability to learn, and our athletic development would inevitably spill over into our daily lives. For the first time, I really saw the relevance of athletics, and saw how training could become a meaningful way of life. The game of athletics expanded beyond physical fitness, recreation, or entertainment; it had become a perfect model for the Game of Life.

The following lessons of nature clarified my approach to movement training . . . and to life.

Principle 1: nonresistance

There are four ways to deal with the forces of life:

• *Surrender* to them fatalistically. Rocks, since they are inanimate, have little choice but to surrender passively to the natural laws.

• *Ignore* them and in ignorance have accidents. Creatures who lack man's perspective are relatively helpless in their ignorance, and are guided only by simple instinct.

• *Resist* them, and create turmoil. Socialized man tends in his cerebralism to resist or struggle with the natural flow of life. Resistance wastes energy and results in various systems of dis-ease.

• *Use* them, and blend with nature. Like the birds that ride the wind, the fish which swims with the current, or the bamboo which bends to absorb the weight of fallen snow, we can make use of natural forces. This is the real meaning of nonresistance. It's been said in many ways: "Don't push the river." "Let it be." "Go with the flow." "When life gives you lemons, make lemonade."

Nonresistance is more than dumb passivity. Any rock is capable of that. It requires great sensitivity and intelligence to flow with the natural laws.

The natural golfer makes intuitive use of the wind, of the direction the grass grows, of the moisture in the air and the curves of the land. He makes use of gravity by letting the club swing in a natural rhythm.

The natural gymnast doesn't "conquer" the apparatus

any more than a mountain climber can "conquer" a mountain; both only learn to blend with the unique forces at play.

The natural tennis player learns to use the texture of the court to his advantage. "Conquering" is the concept of a combative mind, projecting its own turmoil onto the world. There is no resistance in nature; only in the mind of man.

The natural athlete has dissolved any thought of resistance. He sees an opponent in athletic competition as a teacher who will show him his weaknesses and help him to improve . . . and he intends to do the same for his opponent.

An opponent's movement can be used to your advantage through nonresistance. This principle is well-known in the martial arts of judo, t'ai chi, and aikido. "If pushed, pull—if pulled, push." T'ai chi teaches softness in the face of hardness—absorbing, neutralizing, and redirecting force. Aikido teaches blending with another's energy rather than resisting. Problems of daily life can be handled in the same way.

BLENDING: THE MARTIAL ARTS PRINCIPLE OF NO-COLLISION

Test 1.   Stand squarely in front of a friend. Tense your body. Have him push you with one hand as you resist. How does that feel? What happens? (You probably experience opposition—and he is able to control you; he pushes you backward.)

Next, as he pushes again, take a smooth step back under control; just let your body flow backward at the speed he pushes, so he feels as if he's pushing a feather. What does this feel like? (You may experience no opposition, no resistance, no collision. You are in cooperation; you've created harmony. You are in control and, in fact, can even "allow" him to continue his combative gesture so that he falls to the floor.)

Test 2.   Stand with your right leg and right arm extended toward your friend, with both feet rooted lightly to the floor. Breathe slowly in your lower abdomen; relax. Cultivate a feeling of peace and goodwill. As you maintain this spirit, have your friend come toward you rapidly from a distance of about ten feet, with the intent to grab your right arm, which is extended toward him at hip level.

Just as he's about to grab your hand, you whirl around and behind him by taking a smooth quick step with your rear (left) leg, stepping slightly to the side and beyond him as he lunges past, grabbing for the arm that's no longer there. If you do this smoothly, facing your friend as you whirl around him, you'll maintain equilibrium and control while he totters on the edge of balance—and, in fact, you can throw him with just a gentle backward tug on his shoulder as he's passing you. Again, you "win" without resisting.

Test 3. This blending approach of the aikido practitioner can also be applied to potential verbal confrontations. On such occasions, instead of verbal tussling—trying to prove a point, win an argument, overcome another with reason—just sidestep the struggle.

Simply listen—really listen—to your opponent's point; acknowledge the value of what he is saying. Really appreciate it. Then gently ask if there isn't some validity to your view also. In this way, you can learn to blend and apply nonresistance not only to "attackers" but to all of life's little problems and difficult situations.

Remember that *you* create the struggle in your life; *you* create the collisions. It takes two to tango. You can dissolve all struggle through nonresistance.

Nonresistance: psychophysical applications

"For every action there is an equal and opposite reaction." Most of us are familiar with this law and with its physical applications, but not with its psychophysical import: Most of the actions of socialized man are attempts either to push or slow down the river of life rather than flow with things *as they are*. Such action sets up a turbulence, felt in the human body as physical, mental, and emotional *tension*. Tension is a subtle pain, and like any pain is a signal that something is amiss. When you are out of the natural pattern, you will feel this tension. By listening to this message, you can take responsibility for your own activity, which is setting up turbulence—rather than blame life or circumstances.

The common way athletes resist the natural processes is by *trying*. The word "try" itself implies a weakness in the face of a challenge. The moment you try, you are already tense; therefore, trying is a primary cause of error. If you are natural, simply walking to the refrigerator, writing a letter, or watering the flowers, you don't have to *try* to do these things; you just do them easily. Yet when a challenge arises, you begin to *try*.

When competitors feel they are under pressure and begin to try, they often fall apart. Chuang Tzu, a Chinese sage, observed that when an archer is shooting for enjoyment, he has all his skill; when he shoots for a brass buckle, he gets nervous; when he shoots for a prize of gold, he begins to see two targets.

When one of my gymnasts at Stanford told me he was feeling "tremendous pressure" before competitions, I held out my hand and said, "Give me this 'pressure.' Show it to me; then perhaps I can help you get rid of it." Unable to show me this "pressure," he understood that it was his own mental creation, a result of trying too hard.

To illustrate the effect of trying too hard, I ask you to imagine yourself walking across a four-inch plank of wood, suspended a few inches from the ground. No problem, right? Now transport that plank to a height of ten feet . . . over an alligator pond. Suddenly you begin trying harder. It's the same plank but a different mental state.

The law of action-reaction has the effect, as shown above, of setting up mental opposition when you *try*. Thus, athletes who *try* too hard to stretch will only feel the muscles tensing in resistance. Dieters who *try* to diet only get stronger urges for food—or gain back what is lost. Golfers who *try* to wallop the ball only end up topping it into the rough.

The natural athlete *never tries*. His is an easy, relaxed, and naturally progressive approach. In this way, he avoids internal resistance. It is best to learn to sneak up on things.

Be subtle. If you want a child to follow you, take her lovingly by the hand and pull very smoothly, very gently. She'll flow along. If you give her a sudden tug, she'll pull the other way. Our minds often work the same way.

If you play golf, don't swing the club; let it swing. If you're a gymnast, just let the body pirouette. If you play basketball, let the ball go through the hoop. In life, let things happen naturally, based on fortune and the complexities of circumstance. Making things happen only sets up inevitable turbulence. All this may seem to be a semantic game, but it is actually a way of viewing the world and harnessing the forces of nature. No longer trying, you can be free of tension. No longer resisting, you can train full of natural ease.

Every bamboo shoot "knows" how to bend with the wind, but only man has the insight to put up a windmill. Understanding the spirit of nonresistance, you can join in a partnership with nature. This is the first step in becoming a natural athlete.

Principle 2: accommodation

This principle can best be explained as follows:

• *Athletics, like life, develops what it demands.* Development is precisely commensurate with the demand. No demand, no development; small demand, small development; improper demand, improper development.

• *Demand requires motive.* Without internal motivation to energize a demand, there can be no persistent response.

• *Motivation requires meaning.* The motivating factor must correspond to your values in life; it must seem to offer an improvement or benefit that you want.

• *Demand must take the form of progressive overload.* You

must repeatedly and consistently ask of yourself a little more than you're comfortable with, a little more than you are capable of dealing with easily. This leads us to the following:

• *Development* (through overload) *requires a tolerance for failure.* Development inevitably entails a constant stream of "little failures" along the way to your ultimate goals.

• *Tolerance for failure comes from an intuitive grasp of reality and of the natural laws of learning.* Unrealistic expectations mean a frustrated athlete; realism breeds patience. By understanding the natural principles, you develop a realistic and humorous approach to life's temporary little failures.

Training, then, is a process of development through gradually increasing demand. If realistic, gradual demands are made on the body, the body will develop. If equally sensible demands are made for mental and emotional development, then development will take place in these centers too.

Within its natural capacity, the human organism *will* adapt to demands made upon it. This is *accommodation,* which reflects a law that has allowed the human being to evolve and survive through time. Learning is one kind of accommodation, building muscles another kind. All the homeostatic mechanisms of the body—those which regulate balance and stability of body temperature, acidity, or sugar content in the bloodstream—are systems of accommodation.

Even rocks are subject to this law. If you grind a rock with a tool, it will naturally accommodate by changing its shape. But if you try to grind too quickly, the rock may break. We all work in a similar fashion. The demand for change must be gradual—within our capacity. Climbing a mountain is best done in small steps. If you try to do it in huge leaps, the result may be counterproductive.

Accommodation: psychophysical application

Accommodation is a law, as certain as the law of gravity. Yet most of us don't really trust the law, because we have too many conceptual insecurities, too much confusion. We are always wondering, "Can I become good at this?" "Will I be able to accomplish my goal?" "Will I find success?"

Such questions only create tension and weaken our motivation. Be resolute then. Trust in natural law at least as much as you trust your own mental noise.

PROOF OF THE PUDDING

Here's a simple way to see how *accommodation* works automatically:

Choose a physical action that is presently a little beyond your reach. It may be a push-up, a sit-up, a one-arm push-up, a handstand push-up, sitting on the floor with your legs straight out in front of you and touching your toes, running in place for 5 minutes without becoming exhausted, whatever.

Once you've chosen your feat, attempt to perform it several times in the morning and again in the evening. Do this *every day.* With each attempt, you're asking your body to change. Ask politely—don't overdo it. But be consistent.

Set *no* goals of accomplishment, no time limits, no specific number of repetitions you must do each day. (Some days you may feel like doing a little more; other days, less.)

Continue this for a month, and see what happens. Without really trying, you'll find your body complying with your polite request. It's the same with any change you'd like to make in your habits or your life. It just takes a little time and persistence. The body will adapt and accommodate. Ask and it shall be given.

Once you recognize the inevitability of this principle of accommodation, you become responsible, because you know that your success depends upon the demands you are willing to make on yourself. You will also achieve clarity and psychic security, because you will *know* that if you decide to do something that is within your capacity (see Part 2, "Developing Talent") and if you make use of the elements outlined in this book, you *will* succeed, and that's it. You don't wonder whether a rock will fall to the earth if you drop it; why doubt your own success?

Principle 3: balance

Like yourself every athlete recognizes the need for balance. Yet balance is far more than your sense of equilibrium; it is a Great Principle informing every aspect of your body and mind, your daily life and your training. This principle may be simply stated as "Neither too much nor too little."

The athlete who is naturally oriented toward balance moves neither too fast nor too slow, too aggressively nor too passively, too high nor too low, too far to the right nor to the left. (The latter example of balance is even recognized by intelligent politicians.)

Balance determines the correct pace, timing, and accuracy any athlete depends upon. The human body itself depends upon a delicate balance of its body systems. For optimum health, the body must maintain the proper acid-base and blood-sugar levels; its temperature must be neither too hot nor too cold; it must breathe neither too fast nor too slowly; it must be neither too fat nor too lean, neither too muscular nor too emaciated. Even your intake of water and essential nutrients must be balanced. Everywhere we look, we can see the law of balance at work.

This law is the recognition of natural limitations. It is possible, of course, to go beyond the boundaries dictated by this law, just as you can temporarily resist the other natural laws—but there is an inevitable price to pay. Action-reaction eventually takes hold. The odds are "with the house."

Applying your understanding of this principle to your training, you become immune to impatience and frustration, because you recognize that balance implies that for every "up" cycle, there will naturally be a "down" cycle. It would be wholly unrealistic to expect only "ups." Some days are high energy, and others are not. That's how it is. You win some and you lose some. Seeing this, you are no longer enslaved to the mental highs and lows that tend to correspond with the ups and downs of training. Your realism makes you mature and stable and free. As you learn to accept, to ride, and even to enjoy these cycles, they begin to balance themselves.

The natural athlete understands the need to balance the three centers in training. He may focus on physical training for certain periods, but never to the exclusion of developing emotional stability and mental clarity. In the same way you might concentrate temporarily on developing upper-body skills if your ankle was injured, the natural athlete will make use of sluggish and uninspiring physical days by paying more attention to mental and emotional weaknesses as they surface.

Balance: psychophysical applications

As it becomes more clear that the world—and your training—is a psychophysical process, balance takes on even more profound significance, because you discover that physical imbalances are only symptoms of mental and emotional divergence from the natural pattern of living.

The word "centered" is a useful one to describe the natural athlete, because it refers to a state of simultaneous physical, mental, and emotional balance. In fact, the three centers are so intimately connected that an imbalance in one will affect the others. The martial artist knows that if a person is mentally distracted or emotionally upset, he can be pushed over very easily.

Try the following tests in order to discover for yourself the uses—and abuses—of balance.

▷ YOUR PSYCHOPHYSICAL BALANCE

Test 1. **Assuming that you're relatively calm and happy right now, stand up and balance yourself on one leg. (If that's very easy for you, do it with your eyes closed.) Make a mental note of the relative ease of this act.**

The next time you're upset—angry, sorrowful, fearful, or distracted— take advantage of that upset to learn a valuable lesson. Give yourself this same balance test. You'll notice that one of two things will happen: If you are "meditating on your upset," you'll lose your balance easily. If you are "meditating on your balance," you'll lose your upset. Physical balance and emotional upset are like fire and water; they don't mix well.

Test 2. You can take conscious responsibility for any imbalances— physical or psychological—by doing something out of balance on purpose, in order to see it clearly and to control it.

Next time you play golf or tennis or go to your dance lesson, for example, dedicate a certain portion of your time to being consciously off-balance. You will see your game begin to improve afterward.

If you're too much one way, see if you can play at being too much the other way. For example, if you're too timid, try being too aggressive. If your serves veer too far to the right, make an effort to send them too far to the left.

It's going to feel *extremely* awkward, like wearing a suit two sizes too small; nevertheless, it will do you a world of good, because when you play with both sides, you can find the middle and regain your balance.

Imbalances such as those just described often surface in the competitive and training arena. By correcting those which appear in your own case, you enhance many areas of your daily life.

Principle 4: natural order

Natural order accounts for progressive development *through time*. In nature, one season follows another in the proper sequence, without haste. A tree grows from a seedling as an adult grows from an infant. It doesn't work backward, nor can the process be rushed; it's all clocked into the natural order of things.

Only the human being is in a hurry. Our minds race faster than life. Ignoring the law of natural order, we set time goals for ourselves, then rush to reach these arbitrary goals. It's true that we must have some goals; they're essential for movement in life. Without them, we wouldn't get out of bed in the morning. Yet we should not attempt to make rigid goals in *time*. Time goals are unrealistic, because we cannot foresee the future. The longer-range our goals are, the less realistic they will be. We can foresee the direction of our progress, but *not the pace*. Life holds too many surprising twists and turns, and too many changes to second-guess the natural order of things.

We do know that progress is a function of both time and intensity. You can spend less time and more intensity, or more time and less intensity. This must be balanced.

If you train too hard and too intensely—it's called overtraining—you're likely to burn out after a relatively short time of glory, like a shooting star. If, on the other hand, you spend almost no time and very little intensity . . . well, I suggest that you do start to set modest goals.

Whatever cycles you pass through—no matter what your pace—it's best to trust in *natural order*, and enjoy yourself each day, come what may, with all the energy and humor at your command. (Some days, that isn't much, as we all know.)

Humor is a good sign that you have a balanced perspective, reflecting your alignment with the natural order of life's flow. After all, no matter how magnificent our athletic aspirations or achievements, we remain eternally tiny specks in the great universe missing a putt will hardly shake up the cosmos.

Natural order: psychophysical applications

Every one of us at one time or another has probably thought, "I should be doing better—I should be achieving faster." This is often an indicator that we've forgotten the law of natural order. Like the word "try," the word "should" has little place in the mind of the natural athlete. "Should" implies a dissatisfaction with *things as they are.* It is the ultimate contradiction; it's the trembling foundation of neurosis. Your time is too valuable to spend stewing over things that are not.

Of course, whether training is too "intense" or too "easy" depends upon your capacity. As a coach, I always set up an organized program as a general framework, expecting the individual athletes under my guidance to modify it according to their differing capacities.

One good measure of your alignment with the law of natural order is how much you are enjoying training. Certainly there are good and bad periods, but in general, if you push yourself too much, you'll notice that you've lost the original sense of joy which you had as a beginner. The natural athlete is always like a beginner—full of inspiration.

Two Olympic swimmers, one male and the other female, publicly stated that they would be glad when the Olympics were over so they'd never have to look at another swimming pool. (Can you imagine carrying the same attitude through life? "Yes, I've achieved greatness, but I can't wait till it's over . . .") This is an example of an unnatural approach to training which can have negative carry-over in daily life.

Following the natural laws is essential for full enjoyment and natural growth in daily life. You cannot escape the consequences of these laws. There are no tickets given for violations and no jail sentences, but an "outlaw" from nature creates, out of his own ignorance, his own prison. Thus, on our playing fields as in life, we see both prisoners and free men and women.

Balance between pleasure and pain. Become sensitive to the natural order of things. Practice nonresistance by using whatever fortune brings. Then, as the law of accommodation demonstrates everywhere in nature, you will certainly be able to enjoy your personal success.

Perhaps to a small degree, we are all, every one of us, prisoners of self-created limitations. The natural principles give us the first keys to athletic freedom. In the following chapters you will see the uses of these four great principles in transcending illusory self-concepts, breaking down emotional blocks, and developing whole-body talent—all as preparations for your journey up the mountain path.

For now, trust in the natural principles, and they will take care of you.

2 THE POWER OF AWARENESS

Hearing life's lessons

Life is a Great School, and nature is the ultimate teacher—but without awareness you can't hear the "teacher." Awareness transforms life's lessons into wisdom; it can translate confusing circumstances and events into useful knowledge. Awareness, then, is the beginning of all learning.

Learning is a response to a demand to grow—to do something you couldn't do before. The process of learning therefore naturally involves errors. Errors aren't the problem; ignoring or misunderstanding them *is*. In order to correct an error, you must first be *fully* aware of it; then it's inevitably going to be corrected.

The usual way of measuring "how things are going" in your sports activity is by observing the results. In other words, if you win the match, sink the putt, accomplish your goal, then everything seems fine—but if the match is lost or the ball ends in the rough, you know *something* is wrong. Awareness can translate that "something" into specifics.

True awareness is a sensitivity of the entire organism arrived at through sensory feedback, mental clarity, and emotional intuition. If it were merely an intellectual affair, then babies couldn't learn.

If awareness is obstructed or weak, learning does not take place—or if it does take place, it is random and haphazard. Trying to learn a skill without total awareness is like trying to apply a stamp without adhesive—it just won't stick.

In life and training, errors are always with us. We can say that learning a movement skill, or any other skill, is a process of refining errors to the point where they no longer hinder a desired goal. Even in our NASA space program, errors exist—but they have been minimized to an almost invisible tolerance level, like the gymnastics routines of Nadia Comanici and other current wonders. When errors are no longer measurable, even to the most discerning eye, we call that perfection. Smaller errors make the expert.

It's desirable, of course, to be aware of strengths as well as weaknesses. As you become aware of your strong points, you will find confidence, inspiration, motivation, and satisfaction. Yet it is only awareness of *weaknesses* that allows you to strengthen your foundation and consistently improve; therefore, we focus on awareness of error.

Awareness, disillusion, and success

If you've acknowledged that awareness of errors is essential to improvement—and, in fact, is the greatest step in correcting any weakness—you might assume that growing awareness is a pleasant affair. On the contrary, awareness is a disillusioning process and requires the spirit of a warrior.

I remember a phenomenon that occurred during my first

few months of aikido training. This flowing martial art requires relaxation-in-movement even under attack. In the face of this demand for relaxation, I began to notice a great deal of tension in my shoulders. At first I thought that aikido was "making me" tense—but gradually I realized that I was only for the first time becoming aware of tension I had always carried.

Many gymnastics students of mine would tell me how they "used to be better" and how they were "going downhill." This used to worry me . . . until I saw films of them from the year before—and it was obvious that they had radically improved. They were simply much more aware of errors than they were the previous year.

One sure sign of growing awareness is that you "feel" as if you are getting worse. Awareness is literally a disillusioning process, because it cuts through illusion; it entails a momentary drop in self-esteem, a dent in our self-image. No one really likes to look at his weaknesses, so we all have a tendency to resist awareness.

It is important that you understand this phenomenon, because there's a tendency for students to become discouraged and even quit a sport *just* when they are beginning to become aware and proficient—imagining that they are "getting worse."

Whole-body awareness

Most athletes have the courage to see and overcome physical errors, so that one center is developed. The way of the natural athlete, however, is to increase awareness of weaknesses in the *whole* body, or the three centers. This can be supremely difficult unless we're willing to lose face, to see ourselves momentarily in a light that is less flattering than we would wish. We *all* have mental, emotional, as well as physical traits from childhood that are maladaptive, immature, and downright silly. In most people they remain hidden from their own awareness—to surface momentarily in times of upset, pressure, or crisis. Awareness is like sunlight over a dark well. We don't see the little demons lurking there until the light of awareness shines directly overhead; then we notice all these unfortunate qualities in ourselves, and conclude that we're not such magnificent humans after all.

If we resist seeing physical weaknesses a little, we resist awareness of mental and emotional weaknesses a *lot*. There are two very good reasons for this: First, *it's easier to see physical errors*. The results are on a gross level, right in front of us. If we're missing the baseball, for example, it's pretty obvious that we're making an error. Emotional and mental weaknesses are more subtle, harder to see. Second, *we identify more with our minds and emotions than we do with our bodies*. There is a law that what we identify with we tend to defend. We defend our self-image, our loved ones, our values much more ferociously than we defend those things we consider separate from ourselves.

I remember an old cartoon I saw in a magazine. It showed a man pushing a small cart with frozen ice cream inside. He stood listening to a man standing on a platform, sermonizing to a small crowd. The ice-cream vendor's face showed increasing interest and agreement as the speaker said, "Down with Fascism! . . . down with Communism! . . . down with big government! Down with politicians! . . ." But suddenly the vendor's face grew sour, and he walked off, muttering under his breath. The speaker had added, "Down with ice cream!"

You may doubt the fact that we identify with (and defend more intensely) our minds and emotions than our bodies—but do you notice how people feel less awkward talking about their physical illnesses than about an emotional or mental problem? If you tell an athlete he looks clumsy on a particular occasion, he might be a little upset—

but if you tell him he appears to be stupid or immature (corresponding mental or emotional weaknesses), he's far more likely to be upset or defensive. This defensiveness is the primary mechanism of resisting awareness of errors. The natural athlete cannot allow himself such defensiveness; it's too heavy a burden to carry if he is to become light and free.

If you are to become the natural athlete, aligned with the natural laws, you must bring nonresistance to awareness. Open eyes will see the weaknesses, cut through illusion, and transform your errors into whole-body awareness . . . and power. In this way, the athletic arena has tremendous potential for whole-body development, as hidden weaknesses surface in the heat of competition and training.

In understanding our built-in tendency to resist seeing our own foibles and weaknesses, we can see why the process of learning isn't simple for adults. Children, on the other hand, living in an adult world, are used to losing face; making errors is a major part of their lives. Most of what infants *do* is make errors. They wet their pants, fall over, drop things. Yet they have nothing to resist, so the progression of awareness-practice-correction is natural to them. If it were so for us, learning would accelerate rapidly.

What happens to most of us in our athletic endeavors is that we're "sort of" aware of what we're doing wrong—and we "sort of" try for a while to correct it. Often, however, we feel momentarily worse when we try to make corrections based on confused awareness, so we tend to go back to whatever habit patterns we've been accustomed to.

One lady whose husband beat her was relating her marriage problem to a friend. The friend asked her why she just didn't leave the creep and marry someone else who was less violent.

The wife replied, "Oh, well, at least I'm used to him."

We often get beaten by our own habits, but like the battered lady, "at least we are used to them."

The growth of awareness

Awareness, like everything else, is subject to the natural laws. It doesn't "happen" all at once, but develops in a natural order, from gross to subtle. Your own growth of awareness is similar to self-sculpture. First you determine the shape you want to bring out of a stone (your goal). Then you begin hacking and hewing. This "rough cutting" is your general awareness. Later you are ready for the detail work and polishing—the most subtle awareness.

An example of gross awareness is noticing that you sometimes fall down accidentally, or that you tend to have an explosive temper and hit people, or that you often become distracted and forget where you are. An example of subtle awareness is the diver who must pay close attention to the position of his hands and fingers even during a triple somersault, or the yogis who have learned, through close attention to subtle cues, to control internal muscles, glands, and body systems which were previously considered involuntary.

An old samurai warrior knew his time on earth was near an end, and wished to bequeath his sword to the brightest of his three sons. He designed a test.

He had a friend hide just inside the barn, above the doorway, and gave him three bags of rice. He then invited each son inside, one at a time.

The first son, after feeling the rice bag fall on his head, drew his sword and cut the bag in half before it hit the ground.

The second son halved the bag even before it hit his head.

The third son, sensing something amiss, declined to enter the barn—and so earned his father's sword.

We can say that a *beginner* is someone who has not refined his awareness of errors relative to a particular skill. In this sense, we are all beginners, for no matter what we've accomplished, there are always new refinements for which we haven't yet developed subtle awareness. In our journey up the mountain, we're all beginners in new territory.

The Margaret analogy

At Oberlin College, I once had the pleasure of coaching a dedicated diver named Margaret. Her progressive growth of awareness in learning a particular dive parallels the stages we all go through in training—and in daily life.

After her first attempt, she had no awareness of what she had done wrong, and had to rely entirely on my feedback.

After more attempts, she could tell *me* what she had done incorrectly *after* the dive was finished and the errors had been made.

Before long she was becoming aware of her errors *during* the dive.

Finally, her awareness was integrated with body, mind and emotions *before* the dive, and the errors were corrected before they were made. The dive was beautiful.

This example has profound implications for daily life, because we go through the same process in all kinds of learning situations.

There is a great difference between recognizing an error, which comes after a simple explanation, and accepting an error *as an error*, which implies full responsibility for its correction. For an example, there was a young lady on our gymnastics team who was overweight. She *recognized* that she needed to lose her extra fat. She could see it in a mirror. Yet it took her one full year to become *fully aware* of this weakness as an *error*. For a long time she had resisted *seeing* what was obvious to her friends—in the same way alcoholics may go for years without recognizing the obvious.

In athletics or daily life then, a habitual error must be felt, not merely acknowledged verbally, before anyone will generate the motivational impulse to change.

I had a friend named Roger, who talked too much. He practically never stopped talking; maybe he even talked in his sleep. He *knew* that he was a marathon talker—in fact, it was one of his favorite topics of conversation. Yet Roger did not see his habit as an error.

Most of Roger's acquaintances, wanting to be tolerant, never told him that he was an outright bore. One day at a party, in the middle of one of his favorite monologues, a young lady told him he was "deadly boring." She told him that it was impossible to have a dialogue with him and pointed out how people walked away as he approached.

At first Roger was very upset. He had lost face. Before long, he began to notice his talking sprees as an error—after they had ended. Within a few weeks he had begun to notice his compulsive verbalizing *as* he was talking. (In fact, it began to seem that his endless talk was getting worse than ever.) Eventually, Roger remembered to quell his talks before he got going. He became a good listener—and, as these stories go, he ended up marrying the candid lady.

As Roger learned to control his mouth, we can all learn to control our whole body. Awareness is the key, the ability to hear the lessons all around us.

Teachers who understand the progressive growth of awareness need never be impatient with their students, because a wise teacher realizes that telling a student of his errors is a limited form of communication, addressed only to his mind. It takes longer for full awareness to pervade all three centers, giving the emotional impulse, mental clarity, and physical ability to change.

That is how awareness grows in the diver, skier, cellist,

pool shooter, golfer, potter ... and you. Realizing the natural growth of awareness allows you to be your own gentle teacher—and then you are willing to give yourself sufficient time in which to learn.

Feedback aids to awareness

We've all run into a situation where we know that we're making an error, but don't know what it is. In situations like this, it saves time to use an aid to awareness. The following are helpful aids:

The Other Students. The errors and successes of other athletes can serve as lessons and as inspiration.

Students less skilled than you remind you of your own progress—and in the same way you see that these beginners can improve as you did, you understand that you can also continue to improve.

Students who are more advanced serve as examples to copy, which is the way infants learn, and probably the most natural way to learn. Advanced athletes can inspire you by showing that high-level skills *are* accessible.

Visual Feedback. Nothing serves the growth of awareness so instantly and so well as seeing a film or videotape of your own movements. Even a mirror can help you to become realistic about your strengths and weaknesses.

The Teacher. The videotape or film can show you what you look like, but only the teacher can pinpoint the specific errors in order of priority. The teacher is an intelligent feedback aid who can analyze and communicate errors and the ways to correct them.

The teacher has journeyed further up the mountain than you, and can show you how to avoid some of the pitfalls. Throughout history, the teacher has been one of the best sources of feedback in the growth of awareness.

Exaggeration. If you don't have access to films or teachers or videotapes and want a shortcut to awareness, then all you have to do is *deliberately exaggerate* your errors. If you are slicing your golf ball or continually falling in one direction, do it even worse—on purpose. This serves two purposes: First, the error becomes obviou; your awareness grows instantly. Second, your errors become conscious, deliberate, and controlled instead of unconscious. In this way, errors become far easier to correct.

There are some teachers who advocate letting yourself make errors, to cultivate patience and be free from self-criticism. This is very good. But in going beyond this and deliberately repeating the error consciously, you will soon be free of it. *Deliberate* error is no longer an error.

3 PREPARATION

A key to success

Preparation is the foundation for success. Most athletes, however, do not prepare for their journeys. The way most children learn athletics in school is pure Darwinian survival. The teachers run them through their paces, and in the end a few survive to make the varsity. The others are left behind, and often never discover their own potential.

All things in nature have a gestation period and must go through the proper stages to be formed. Natural learning works the same way. The natural athlete makes use of this natural way—beginning with *thorough* preparation.

Complete preparation is both the most difficult and the most important part of any learning process. Ninety-five percent of making Chinese vegetables is in the preparation: heating the wok to just the right temperature, cleaning and fine-slicing the vegetables, making sure they are crisp—then the cooking is easy.

In painting a car, you must first go through the arduous work of cleaning the body, sanding it, filling in nicks, pounding out dents, sanding again, cleaning again, masking and priming—then, swish! the painting is easy. What would the paint job look like if you didn't prepare the auto properly first? It would look like the usual athlete—both are uneven, bruised looking, and quick to show wear and tear.

Any obstructions you have ever encountered or may someday encounter are a direct result of insufficient or improper preparation. For example, an athlete who has developed strength but ignored the need for suppleness will tend to compensate for his lack of flexibility with more strength. It may appear to "work," but this imbalance will, at some point, block further learning.

To further understand the necessity of preparation, picture an iceberg floating in the sea. The visible tip of the iceberg represents the skills you actually show in performance or competition. The remainder of the iceberg represents your preparation. It may not be visible from the surface, but without it, the showy part would turn over and sink.

Learning is much like building a house. *The skills* are the visible part of the *upper-house structure. Physical talent* makes up the *foundation* of the house. *Mental and emotional talent*—such qualities as freedom from self-concept, one-pointed concentration, and stable motivation—are the *ground* on which the house and foundation stand.

The foundation of a house and the ground beneath the foundation aren't very flashy. No one drives by a house and says, "Wow! Will you look at that classy foundation!" Yet without a solid foundation on stable ground, even the most beautiful house is unstable and will eventually fall.

One particular high-school gymnastics coach developed more Olympians than any other I know of. His secret:

preparation. He made the young men under his guidance spend their first two years working almost exclusively on the qualities of talent: suppleness, strength, speed, relaxation, and the learning of proper fundamentals. It was slow and difficult for the team, which didn't show much for a few years. Many gymnasts quit. The ones who understood, stayed—and the ones who stayed became some of the finest gymnasts in the country. One of these young men was my teammate, who later beat me at the national championships. This same approach will work for any movement activity, because it is aligned with the natural laws of learning.

We all would like to find shortcuts up the mountain path. Consider two spaceships, about to race to the most distant point in the galaxy. Spaceship A has an impatient captain and crew. They take off first—half fueled, missing some provisions—but they get a long head start. Spaceship B remains standing until all preparations are complete, with a full supply of fuel. They seem far behind.

I leave it to you to guess who will ultimately win.

Charting a proper course

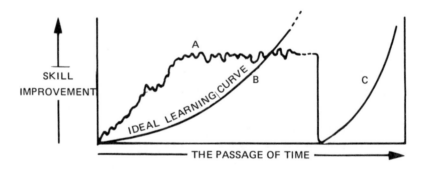

The above chart illustrates three possible learning patterns.

Curve A shows the hasty, random, up-and-down learning

curve of the usual athlete. He improves rapidly at first, but as the skill level becomes more complex, weaknesses begin to have a greater influence. Due to insufficient grounding in preparation—and therefore a weak foundation—the up-and-down cycles are amplified, and progress eventually levels off.

If you reach this point, you might believe you're "too old" or that you've reached your "potential." Motivation may wane. You may feel that "other things in life are really much more important" and eventually retire.

Curve B is the path of the total athlete. At first he appears to improve very slowly. The path is initially difficult, with little to show. This athlete is working "below the water-line," developing a hidden foundation. Gradually but surely, the curve begins to turn upward, until progress accelerates at a rapid, consistent, and almost effortless pace.

Curve C is really the most important, because it represents a second wind for most of us. If your preparation has been insufficient and you have been stuck on a plateau, you can duplicate the path of the natural athlete by first going back for a time—perhaps a few months—to do intense work on the talent foundation (see following chapters) and funda-mentals. Allow yourself to progress very slowly. In a relatively brief time, your progress will begin to accelerate upward again, passing your old marks.

Step-by-step preparation

Whether you are concerned with physical, mental, or emotional preparation—and as you'll learn in future chap-ters, all three of them are crucial—a step-by-step approach to the task at hand can be the key to success. You may be trying to work out a complicated problem in physics, you may be job-hunting, you may want to do a back flip in midair. For most of us, each of these accomplishments may seem overwhelmingly difficult. But each of them can be broken down into a series of small steps, gradually and methodically leading to the final goal. If you concentrate on the impossibility of the achievement, you'll almost certainly fail. If you learn to focus your energies on each of the intermediate steps, you will make the process itself much more manageable and enjoyable and, almost without noticing your progress, you will find yourself nearer and nearer to the goal. Anything and everything in life can be broken down into its component parts, and the more adept you become at this preliminary to accomplishment, the more you'll amaze yourself by what you can do.

The illusion of difficulty

"Difficulty" has no absolute meaning; it is only relative to your preparation. If you're prepared—if you've developed all the necessary physical, mental, and emotional qualities—then nothing will be difficult for you.

A common experience for the usual athlete is to find learning easy at first but more difficult as time passes. This increasing difficulty is such a common pattern that we accept it as normal. Yet it is not the natural pattern; it is only a reflection of insufficient preparation.

The natural athlete is one who has developed his talent from the outset, making learning easier as time passes.

In order to avoid falling onto path A, that of the usual athlete, we might take a look at the primary reasons anyone chooses this way:

• He might not appreciate the importance of thorough preparation.

• He might not know what thorough preparation consists of.

- He may be in a hurry, seeking shortcuts, because he lacks a realistic map of understanding.
- Lacking confidence, he may avoid a path that appears slower at first and promises few immediate rewards.
- He may have a teacher who falls into one of the above categories.

Many coaches and teachers allow or even encourage shortcuts in order to "keep the students interested" or because it's "more practical." Immediate competitive pressures and deadlines aggravate this tendency.

Beginning students cannot be expected to have a complete understanding of the training process and priorities. Therefore, an intelligent and patient teacher is one of the most important aspects of your training. Choose with great care.

Choosing a teacher

The teacher is your guide along a mountain path. Some guides are familiar with the lowlands; others can show you the entire way. The best guide has seen all his own weaknesses, and therefore has insight into yours; he can show you the obstacles, but also point out the interesting side roads and beautiful scenery along the way. If a guide insists that you travel exactly the same path he did, then his knowledge is limited. Find a guide who can assess your qualities and find the best way for you. A fine teacher, filled with natural awareness, can be a beacon to help light your way.

Second only to parents, movement teachers can have a profound influence on a student's self-concept and outlook on life. A genuine teacher conveys useful lessons of living through a movement form. An average teacher just teaches skills. Beware of knowledgeable, skillful teachers who can develop "winning" teams, but at the same time smother the fundamental enjoyment and freedom of athletics.

If you can appreciate the importance of a good teacher, pick one for yourself or for your child with the same care you'd use to pick a surgeon. You wouldn't want to be operated on by a mediocre surgeon—even if he *is* a nice guy, has his office right near your house, or charges a few dollars less. Yet this is how many people pick movement teachers. Finding a superior teacher for yourself or your child is worth some research, and is money well spent— because an inspired teacher can be a positive influence that a child, or an adult, will remember the rest of his life.

Teaching is an *art of communication*. If one teacher possesses 100 volts of knowledge but can effectively convey only 20 volts to his students, he will be less effective than a teacher who has 50 volts of knowledge plus the ability to convey it all.

If a teacher has a great competitive record with many championships, this *may* be very positive, because such a teacher has traveled far on his own mountain—and his accomplishments may inspire his students, who are more likely to listen with respect and attention, and follow through with his directions. However, do not be overawed by a competitive record or a whole list of advanced degrees. *The important thing is not what a teacher knows, but what his students know; not what he can do, but what they can do.*

A good teacher can speak the language of the intellect— words—and communicate clearly so the student understands.

An excellent teacher can speak the language of the body—by showing the muscles, bones, and nerves how something should feel if done properly.

A great teacher speaks the language of the emotions—by inspiring and motivating, and rekindling the original love of the activity with which you began.

The master teacher can do all three.

There are gifted teachers out there somewhere—and they may be found in unexpected places. Remember that the best teachers not only teach a subject—they convey principles of living *through* a subject.

The preparation of children: a note to loving parents

. . . and a time to every purpose under the heaven.
—*Ecclesiastes 3:1*

As you look around yourself at the haste and rushing of today's time-schedule world, you can understand why you, too, tend to be in a hurry now and then. Our haste spills over onto the children—and nowhere is this more apparent than in children's athletics. Perhaps before long we will see Diaper League Championships, complete with preschool cheerleaders. Instead, however, I would recommend the following considerations:

Movement play for young children (and even infants) is wonderful. It stimulates them, exercises them, and opens their vital little bodies to a means of enjoying and discovering their relationship to the natural laws. However, skills aren't important for children. What is important is that they learn:

• to feel good about their bodies.

• to feel success in their early endeavors (therefore they need relatively easy tasks).

• to learn the enjoyment of active movement which stems from accomplishment.

• to develop confidence from completing tasks.

Success should be measured by a child's beaming smile—not by parental goals or aspirations.

Children need to play with other children, on child-sized equipment in a child-sized environment of color and softness and safety. One early injury, fear, or failure can affect the child for a long time.

I don't personally recommend private lessons (especially if Mom or Dad is the teacher). A well-intentioned adult may give patient and skilled instruction, but what the child perceives is a larger, infinitely more capable adult model whom he cannot hope to emulate successfully. This can be very discouraging for a child. (On the other hand, watch how the child delights in seeing Mom or Dad fumble, and how he laughs with glee when you let him feel stronger or smarter than you.) A good learning environment for a child is within a small group of other children—some more, and some less skilled.

Early play can help prepare a child for easier development later on—but the focus is on early *play* which feels good, not intense training. It is also best to avoid a competitive emphasis too early. Later on, it has value, but only if the child is prepared by an early cooperative emphasis.

Children can begin different kinds of movement training at different ages. The main determining factors are the development of the bones and joints, the attention span, and *natural interest*. If your child is interested in anything—whether or not *you* have any interest in it—let him try it, if he's willing to make a commitment for at least three months. On the other hand, if you start your child in a direction only you are interested in, be prepared for eventual disappointment.

If your child is motivated—and if he has been prepared well—it only takes about four or five years of serious training to approximate his highest level of achievement. The later years only bring subtle refinements and stabilize his attainments. Thus, you don't need to start a "budding Olympian" in long workouts before he's out of diapers.

Overinvolved parents who, in their loving enthusiasm, want to help their youngster "a little too much" often can do as much harm as good. *Too* much interest can set up confusion in the child and weaken his core of motivation, because he's never sure whether he's participating from his own native interest or living out a parental fantasy. He will feel this internal contradiction no matter *what* his parents assure him—because children can be acutely sensitive (far more than they appear to be) and are quick to see through the social lie that we may believe.

What you *can* offer your child is financial support, transportation to classes, mild interest, and emotional support. It's great to go to a game occasionally, but if you get too zealous or wildly excited when he wins, he's going to feel that you're equally disappointed in him when he loses.

Athletics, games, and movement play are as good for children as they are for adults—but training *must* follow the natural principles to reap the greatest benefits. Preparation—both physical and psychological—is essential if your child is to receive the full benefits of his journey.

Part Two

The Groundwork

Developing talent

There's a common belief that talent is inborn. This belief accounts for the usual programs of training, which only casually, randomly, and haphazardly deal with the *foundation* of potential— the qualities of talent. Most of us simply do the best with what we already have.

It's true, of course, that there are certain inherited traits such as body height, which can give you a head start in sports like basketball—but you can develop those other key qualities that enable you to shine in your sport.

The athletic stars you see on television, who have survived years of training to approach their peaks, haven't necessarily followed the course I will outline. Yet they are a product of natural selection; you don't see the many athletes who drop out, because they lacked the qualities that the superstars developed at random in their youth. Every time I teach at a gymnastics camp, I see boys and girls practicing diligently, who meet frustrating obstacles due to insufficient preparation—because they lack qualities of strength or suppleness or emotional stability or mental clarity.

It is possible just to play the game and let the necessary qualities emerge as time passes. This, in fact, might seem to be the most natural approach. It would be,

except for one catch: We all like to feel successful; thus, we enjoy working and showing our strong points—and tend to avoid practicing our weak points in the heat of the game. Our usual pattern is to let our strengths compensate for our weak areas. This seems to work for a while, but eventually we develop imbalances, which block further progress. By emphasizing *talent drills* early in our career and before every game, we can avoid the need for compensations and build a well-rounded foundation.

Developing talent *first* saves a great deal of time. I remember one young man who, in high school, decided that he wanted to become a top gymnast. He asked advice from every coach he could find. He was told to begin by developing strength, suppleness, and correct fundamentals before he concentrated on skill development. He set out to follow this advice. No one heard from him for about a year—then "all of a sudden," he started to impress people. He recently graduated from the University of California at Berkeley, which he attended on an athletic scholarship, as one of the nation's finest gymnasts.

No matter what you imagine your limitations to be—no matter what your body looks or feels like now, even if you've been in a slump for a year—if you're willing to undergo the initiation necessary to develop your talent, you will become a natural athlete. All the qualities are within you, they are native to you. In some areas, you may have to direct more energy and time than someone else in order to bring out the proper qualities, but you absolutely have the capacity to do it.

Since we all intuitively understand the value of preparation, this advice may seem obvious. Yet few of us *act* on the basis of our understanding—either because we're in a hurry to achieve skills, or because the developmental drills don't seem to be much fun. We all like immediate gratification.

Therefore, to encourage a realistic approach to training, it's been my intent to emphasize the intelligence of patience and the wisdom of preparation.

A natural response at this point might be, "Sure, preparation helps; developing talent seems like a great idea—but what *are* the specific qualities of mental, emotional, and physical talent?" The answer to that question is the topic of the next three chapters.

The mind leads the body.
—Koichi Tohei, aikido master

Golf is twenty percent technique
and eighty percent mental.
—Ben Hogan, golf professional

4 MENTAL TALENT

Releasing the brakes

Perhaps you remember occasions when you were lost in thought. Someone may have been talking with you—and you realized that you "hadn't heard a thing." At another time you might even have driven through a red light without seeing it. On occasions like these, your ears were functioning and your eyes were open, but your *attention was captured* by thought. Your attention can go in two fundamental directions: outward, to the world of energy and movement, or inward, to thoughts. For most of us, attention randomly bounces back and forth from inner concerns to outer realities.

The psychotic individual is an extreme example of

someone completely "lost in thought." For him, the habit of turning attention inward is so compelling that he's lost the capacity to maintain contact with reality as we know it. In contrast, most of us are able to direct our attention out into the world with relative consistency—far more effectively than the psychotic. Yet to a lesser degree, we're subject to the same liability. We're all bound, at one time or another, by episodes of obsessive thought.

If you sit down in a quiet room and close your eyes, you'll soon begin to notice many subtle stimuli that are normally below your conscious recognition. You may notice little aches or areas of tension. You'll become aware of your breathing and the expansion/release of your diaphragm and chest muscles. You'll notice the rhythmic beating of your heart. And there are far more subtle internal displays that may arise, even of sound and light. But above all else, you may be surprised to notice the stream of reactive thought that flows on and on and on.

The natural athlete has learned to focus his attention on the matter at hand, in the present moment. Thoughts may come and go, but his attention is not bound by inward distractions of any kind. Most of us are subject to the pattern of random attention, floating back and forth between the world and our inner content—the stream of reverie, fantasy, concerns, plans, fears, anger, expectations, sorrow, regrets, and rehearsals.

The adult mind is full of compulsive, random (and usually problematic) thinking. The most "charged" or disturbing thoughts take the shape of worry, fear, and anger, and such thoughts impose tension on the body. You can test the truth of this in your own experience.

In athletics and in daily life, the source of our discontent is this primitive habit of allowing our attention to drift to reactive thoughts. For example, if something happens which we don't like (because of beliefs we hold), we become angry. We don't necessarily want to become angry—we may even know it's not good for our health to become angry—but we get angry just the same. We've all experienced compulsive reactions of jealousy, sorrow, worry, and fear in the same way. We don't *want* to become obsessed with such thoughts, but we do nevertheless.

It may *seem* as if various wrongs in the world are the source of our disturbances—but if we examine our habit patterns very closely, we see that mental resistance-to-the-stream-of-life is the seed of our discontent. My wife and I returned from a trip to find that our car had been stolen. It would have been very easy to blame the car thieves or the circumstances for any upset we might have felt—but it was too obvious that our own *reaction* to one of life's little surprises was actually causing turmoil. This reaction was in the form of preoccupation with thoughts about what had happened. In seeing this, we were able to take responsibility for our own compulsive reaction and stop blaming circumstances for our disturbance. Car thieves could only steal our car; it was our own obsession with problematic thoughts that could upset us. We decided not to let them get the better of us and we gave those thoughts "no mind." That evening, we were laughing, ready to see what turned up next.

Meditation student
speaking to teacher: I'm feeling upset.

    Teacher: You're reacting to a passing thought. Forget it.

    Student: I can't seem to forget it.

    Teacher: Then let it go.

    Student: I can't let it go, either.

    Teacher: Then just drop it.

    Student: I can't drop it!

    Teacher: Well, then I guess you'll just have to throw it out.

Mental talent emerges as you gain facility in dissolving archaic habit patterns, so that you no longer feel compelled to pay attention to the obstructions and limitations which are primitive creations of your own mind. All rigid mental patterns manifest themselves as tension and physical symptoms. The usual athletic practice is to deal with and work to overcome the physical symptoms—stretching to become loose, practicing relaxation techniques to let go of tension, and so on. However, such working on symptoms is a remedial activity. There is no profound value, for example, in stretching for twenty minutes a day and letting an uncontrolled mind tie the body in knots the rest of the time. Techniques of stretching and relaxation can be very useful and, in fact, are central elements of physical talent—but first we have to deal with the *source* of physical symptoms.

There is an amusing sanity test. A door swings open before you, and you see a sink full of water. The stopper is in, and the water is running. The water begins to pour over the sink's edge. The "sanity test" is whether you turn off the water or run for a mop. In learning to deal with the mind and develop your mental talent, you are turning off the water. Unfortunately, we see many athletes out there training diligently at mopping up.

One effective way to see your own mental condition more clearly is by comparing it with the state of the infant. The tiny baby gathers and stores many impressions of the movement and energy he perceives in the world. But because he has no words, because he has no complex associations, beliefs, opinions, values, and attitudes *relative* to those impressions, he doesn't think much *about* anything. The infant doesn't cogitate, ruminate, or contemplate—and he doesn't philosophize, conceptualize, or theorize either. His attention is entirely focused outward, in the present moment.

Thus, the very young child is still relatively free from

the complex fears, angers, attachments, expectations, plans, biases, self-imagery, and self-criticism that is characteristic of the adult mind.

The baby is a natural athlete in his clarity, his relaxation, his sensitivity and openness to the environment, in his simple, direct approach to life. He's free of mental reaction or resistance. These traits account not only for the relatively astounding learning abilities of the infant, but for his innate charm and attractiveness. The same traits account for the effectiveness of the natural athlete.

Beginning his life as a movement master, his mind free of meaning, the child is naturally happy in his pristine ignorance. It's only when he becomes immersed in meanings and preconceptions that natural learning is inhibited.

There are several ways to approach the mind's powerful influence on movement. We begin by examining four obstructions which seem to plague most of us, at one time or another. They are *illusory self-concept, fear of failure, destructive self-criticism, and lack of one-pointed attention.* The following sections deal with these key problem areas.

Illusory self-concept

The self-fulfilling prophesy is named for a common psychological phenomenon. What it describes is how our progress in life tends to be consistent with our expectations. If you expect or believe something—that you are a super dancer, that you aren't very likable, that you are a whiz kid at math—you will set in motion many psychological processes that tend to make your expectations come true.

Self-concept is a fundamental self-fulfilling prophesy. Your level of achievement will rise with your self-concept.

This applies to any field of endeavor. If you expect to do

poorly, you will be less motivated, less interested; you'll put in less time and energy—and will thus perform poorly.

A new salesman was given a one-hundred-square mile area in which to sell shoes. The first year, he generated $10,000 worth of business. His boss was so pleased, he doubled the man's area the next year. Nevertheless, the salesman still sold only $10,000 worth of shoes. Upset, the boss cut his area to half its original size. That year the salesman still sold $10,000 worth of shoes.

He had a $10,000-a-year self-concept.

Every time a new group of children or adults begins one of my gymnastics classes, I see them acting out roles based upon their self-concept. A few people play the role of class leaders, get in front of the line, and show what they can do. Others may stand quietly at the end of the line, making remarks like "Oh, I'm such a klutz."

You have a different self-concept with respect to the many activities in daily life. You probably have a fairly high self-concept in athletics (or you wouldn't be very motivated to participate); you may have a lower one in auto mechanics or bookkeeping or painting or writing.

What I want to demonstrate is that it is only a self-concept—no more solid than a ghost, no more real than the shadow of a shadow. Self-concept is an illusion that has been imposed upon you long ago, overshadowing your every endeavor until you can see it for what it is and cut through it.

One way of battling destructive self-concepts is to write down a list of fifty qualities or abilities you possess, or activities you engage in or might wish to engage in (i.e., sports, cooking, bookkeeping, taking care of children, love-making, auto mechanics, etc.). Once the list is complete, rate yourself on a 1–10 scale, 1 being totally inept, 10 being world class.

I emphasize: You don't have to write down only those activities you actually do—in fact, it may be more helpful to include many activities you avoid. Once you've rated yourself, take a look at this reflection of your self-concept.

Look at the low self-ratings. Do you enjoy any of those activities? Have you ever really put effort in these areas to become proficient? Is there any good reason you *really* couldn't become very good at any of these skills? (Remember that people with no arms have become excellent painters; one-legged men have become fine diving performers; blind people have excelled at running marathons and bouncing on the trampoline.)

The final step in this exercise: When you finish this chapter, sit quietly and consider the main points about illusory self-concept. Look over your list and self-ratings one more time—then, with great pleasure, burn the list.

Through insight into the illusory nature of your self-concepts, you can overcome self-imposed limitations. Then, and only then, can your techniques or training have any real momentum.

In order to know your enemy, remember your childhood, when you were free of self-concept. As a child, you were *pure potential* and could learn anything within human capacity. You had within you the seeds of being a physician, an attorney, an engineer, an expert craftsman, a dancer, an artist, or an Olympian. It never occurred to you that learning was difficult. You were free from assumed limitation.

Four-year-old Jenny decided that she wanted to learn to fly. It seemed elementary enough to her—even birds could do it. She stood on the couch and jumped, her arms flapping. Her first attempt was not entirely successful.

Jenny reasoned that since birds have feathers, this must be the missing ingredient. She found a feather in the yard. Holding it in her little hand, she leaped again into the air. She told her father that the feather had "definitely helped."

In letting his daughter attempt to fly from the couch, my friend was allowing her to explore safely her *natural* powers and limitations. In this way she was able to gain a balanced, realistic view of her abilities; not one imposed upon her by other people's expectations. When I asked her father why he hadn't just saved her some effort and explained to her that "little girls and boys can't fly," he replied, smiling, "How could I know? I might have been wrong."

When you were very young, you were free to learn, open to anything, like Jenny. As you grew, however, you began to get impressions that you were "good" at some things and "bad" at others—because you were praised and blamed, or because you misunderstood the situation.

It was in kindergarden painting class that I made my first picture of a tree. It looked like a green lollipop, since it was my first try. Then I looked around at the paintings of the other children, and to my disappointment, *their* paintings looked like *trees.* I didn't understand that they had drawn many more trees than I. I didn't realize that, if I continued to practice as much as they had, my trees might look even more leafy than theirs. But I gave up too soon. Then and there, I decided that I was not a good painter.

Little Sammy formed a self-concept in another way. He was reaching for a glass of milk. Being three years old, he misjudged the distance and knocked the milk over. His mother, momentarily upset, said, "Oh, clumsy child!" This word "clumsy" was new to Sammy. He figured it had something to do with milk.

On another occasion, it happened again—but this time, with juice. "Clumsy!"

"Ah," Sammy reasoned. "It doesn't mean milk, it means *spilling* that makes me clumsy." Sammy formed the idea that he was clumsy—and soon, he had several dozen glasses of spilled liquid and a few falls down flights of stairs to *prove* it.

The undesirability of a low self-concept may seem obvious, since it limits our achievement. Yet, an unrealistically high self-concept has its own unique problems. A young child who is praised for everything gets used to being praised. Praise represents positive energy and attention which all children crave. He will strive to maintain this praise as much as possible. He may even develop precocious abilities. This child's sense of self-worth will depend upon achievement and success. He expects himself to succeed—and projects this onto the world, so that it seems everyone else expects him to succeed too. There can be tremendous psychic pressure not to let the world down. This pressure can create brilliant students, star athletes . . . and suicides.

Unrealistically high *or* low self-concept is debilitating. The best self-concept is none at all. A child raised in a home relatively free from exaggerations of praise or blame will just take a realistic, experimental, and persevering approach to his pursuits, without undue psychic pressure. He achieves naturally, in good time, with ordinary enjoyment.

Well, we're not children anymore, and we *do* have an ample supply of self-concepts, relative to our activities. Whenever you feel underconfident or confused about a specific endeavor—or if you are feeling *pressure to do well* —you can be sure that an arbitrary self-concept is imposing itself on your life, shattering your ease and enjoyment. The next time this occurs, you can surrender to it, you can ignore it, you can resist it, or you can use it. If you surrender to it, your past will become your future. If you ignore it, the self-concept will continue to have subtle effects. If you resist it, you'll waste energy. *Use* it fully. Experience its psychic force . . . then cut through it by *changing your act*. Learn to do what you didn't believe you could do, and the word "can't" will lose its power over your life.

When we say, "I'm not interested in doing that," what we often *feel* behind that statement is "I can't do well at that." When "can't" loses its force, you would be amazed at how many things you suddenly become interested in.

It's of great benefit to try on new possibilities in your life. You can begin this in a very simple way. Make a positive statement to yourself—for example, "I am an accurate putter." "I am a courageous gymnast who performs even better under pressure." "I always remember names and faces of the people I meet." "I enjoy not smoking, and don't need to smoke."

These statements may seem like bold-faced lies. However, in making the statement, you are creating *psychic dissonance*—a kind of internal pressure between the statement and your actions. Given certain laws of the psyche (based upon accommodation), there will be a pressure to change and reconcile the activity with the statement. You don't have to believe the statement or hypnotize yourself. Just say it, think it, and try to feel it a few times in the morning and evening and before you train. Then forget it and just do what you do. Persist—and all your actions will begin to change. As your actions change, illusory limitations will begin to dissolve. Success breeds success, because it undermines assumed limitation.

Remember always that the law of accommodation is stronger than your illusory self-concept. Don't be so sure you are limited. If you train properly, you *will* improve.

Transcending self-concept is the first real step in becoming a natural athlete.

Fear of failure

Failure is an integral part of the learning process; it's a natural signpost, a guide, an aid to further progress. In order to learn, you must see what's failing, and clearly take it into account. Most of us, when still young, were taught to fear failure—especially public failure—and to avoid it at all costs. Therefore, we have built-in mechanisms of defense against failure. *Fear* is often the "fire" under many hard-working students and athletes. Another common defense against failure is "not really trying." The athlete who appears to be lazy may simply be unmotivated. But why is he unmotivated? Often, the answer is that he doesn't really believe he can do well. Thus, if he doesn't succeed, he can always feel, "I could have done really well if I'd really tried." The pressure from fear of failure is relieved.

Fear of failure produces a vicious circle—and results in the occurrence of what was most feared. It works this way: Fear produces tension. Tension constricts the blood flow, slows the reflexes, produces shallow breathing, results in general contraction of opposing muscle groups, and can even affect eyesight. All this obstructs effective movement, resulting in probable failure.

To break this circle, all you need to do is make peace with failure. It is not your enemy. But it isn't enough merely to tolerate failure. "Tolerate" means to endure something; you have to *appreciate* failure in order to make use of it. Then, ironically, it ceases to distract you.

When you are learning something, give yourself a couple dozen errors for free. Sometimes, miss on purpose, just to stay loose and keep a balanced perspective.

The natural athlete laughs at failure. He recognizes that balancing success with failure is nature's way. The greatest inventors, artists, and athletes of all time failed many, many times. Babe Ruth was the home-run king. He was also the strike-out king.

You can impress this principle upon yourself with the following exercise—a cinch physically but a challenge psychologically. Fail on purpose. If you're a salesman, blow your next sales attempt. Just have fun and don't give a damn. Double your golf score. Make mistakes you'd normally fear making. Have fun with failure and see if the sky falls in. (It won't.) Soon you'll improve by accident.

Destructive self-criticism

If babies carried around the same tendency toward self-criticism that adults do, they would never learn to walk. Can you see an infant learning to walk, falling, and stomping the floor, "Damn! Screwed up again!" Such a baby might try to walk in frustration and anger for a few months, then give up in disgust. Fortunately, babies are free of self-criticism. They treat failure the same as success; they just keep practicing.

Self-criticism is a learned habit pattern, which usually begins in childhood, since kids naturally make errors and are often the target of destructive criticism.

There are only three causes of error in the world:

1. negative (or unconscious) habit patterns;

2. lack of information or experience;

3. the fact that no one is perfect all the time.

There are two kinds of criticism:

1. constructive: "You were a little too high on that one; try swinging lower on the next."

2. destructive: "That's all wrong—boy, was that *dumb!*"

If you received destructive criticism as a child, it is very likely that your young psyche used the most available defense; you *internalized* that criticism—that is, you began to criticize *yourself* severely, so that others would refrain from doing so. This defense of childhood usually "works"—it *does* tend to avoid criticism from parents, brothers, sisters, or playmates. Yet this archaic habit is no longer useful; if you criticize yourself, you're still carrying around that parent, brother, sister, or playmate who was so unkind to you.

You may not be fully aware that you are a victim of your own self-criticism, since you won't always yell or kick yourself. Sometimes it takes subtle forms, such as a generalized impatience or frustration or depression with your actions.

We use self-criticism on ourselves in the same way others once used criticism on us—as punishment for errors. People who criticize themselves share a belief that if they punish themselves in this way, they will improve. Just the opposite is true. If you criticize-punish yourself after making an error, the psychological scoreboard is even: "One error, one punishment." You are free to make the same error again. By *not* criticizing yourself, you are taking responsibility and are *less* likely to repeat the error.

Instead of fighting yourself, see if you can be your own best friend, like Jack, the happy-go-lucky golfer:

On the seventeenth tee, Jack accidentally hit a slice; it flew in an increasing curve, out over the rough, past the drinking fountain, and clear over the golf-course fence. Shrugging his shoulders, Jack teed up again and continued down the fairway.

As he finished his putt on the eighteenth green, a fire

---

chief and two policemen ambled up to him. A crowd of onlookers began to watch.

"Were you the guy," said the police captain, "who sliced a ball over the fence on the seventeenth fairway?"

"Sure did," Jack replied. "But what the heck, it was only a thirty-five-cent ball."

"Listen, fella. That thirty-five-cent ball went through the windshield of a truck. The truck crashed into a tree and blocked the passage of eight fire trucks going to a three-alarm fire. Five buildings burned down, and the people narrowly escaped. What are you going to do about that?"

Jack thought a moment in silence, then replied, "Well, I guess I'll have to move my grip a little to the right."

Like Jack, be constructive. Be gentle with yourself. If you will not be your own unconditional friend, who will be? If you are playing an opponent and you are also opposing yourself—you are going to be outnumbered.

Maintain an attitude of *unconditional self-worth*, free from self-criticism. You can agree that it is cruel and unnecessary to tell someone else, "You are really stupid—what a klutz—you should give up—you keep making the same mistakes—you'll never be any good!" If you would never say those things to anyone else, *why not pay yourself the same courtesy?*

One-pointed attention

There is tremendous power in *total attention* to the matter at hand. But such attention is a relatively rare occurrence. When an athlete has one-pointed attention, he feels really "on." You may have experienced this kind of ecstatic security. When skiers and surfers feel it, they know they won't fall. Golfers in this state can almost literally "see" energy lines from the ball to the hole. Tennis players seem to anticipate what is going to happen before it happens.

For most of us, most of the time, our attention is diffused—distracted by thoughts that arise in the moment, our minds half on what we're doing, half on thoughts *about* what we're doing, or on daydreaming at random. For most of us, then, our efforts in athletics and daily life tend to lack real immediacy and force.

Hypermotivation

Under hypnosis, or in states of hypermotivation—like the mother who lifted the rear of an auto off her injured child— people can manifest extended capacity which comes from one-pointed attention, free of any internal distraction. One-pointed focus, more than brute strength, is what allows the Olympic champion weight lifters to lift more than ever before. The same quality of attention frees you, for the moment, from any thought of self-concept, criticism, or fear; thus, you're also freed of shyness, timidity, or inhibition. Freedom from mental distraction is *power*. On the other hand, even a subtle distraction can affect the body:

Ask a friend to stand comfortably with his arms at his sides. Ask him to tense one arm, locking it straight and clenching his fist, with his arm pointed downward along the side of his body. Tell him you are going to try to pull his arm away from his body, sideways, for a foot or two. Do that, and notice the amount of effort required for you to pull the arm out.

Next, tell him that you are going to wave your hand in front of him, with a zigzag motion downward, without touching him, and then you'll try immediately again to pull his arm outward as you did the first time. Proceed to do this.

Do you notice the difference? What happened to his mental focus when you made the distracting hand motion?

If your friend's attention can be distracted in this way, imagine what mental distractions can do to your performance.

Athletic training is the best school for one-pointed concentration because it demands your full attention in the present. Like the nearly unstoppable runs of O. J. Simpson or the absolute control of Nadia Comanici, you can achieve the ability to follow through, no matter what distractions assail you.

In order for a gymnast to maintain perfect balance on the beam, she must keep her mind squarely over the beam. If a gymnast falls off the beam, her mind has already fallen off. Before a football player can be stopped, his attention must be captured. Any good tackle knows that some runners are more difficult to stop than others, and that it's not just a matter of physical conditioning—it is a matter of mental training.

The following exercise can show you the difference between weak attention-intent, and total one-pointedness:

▷ ─────────────────────

Test 1. **Stand and squarely face a friend from a distance of about 10 feet. His feet are shoulder-width apart, each the same distance from you. Now, feeling timid, walk in a straight line, as if to brush past his right side. As you are about to pass him, he lifts up his right arm directly in front of your chest. Let your mind stop at the arm that is held in front of you.**

Test 2. **This time, do everything exactly the same, with one mental difference. Walking the same speed, project your attention with force a thousand miles in front of you. Therefore, you pay no attention to your friend's arm as it is raised; your mind and your forward motion continue right through the arm as if it isn't there; relaxed, positive, centered. What do you experience this time?**

In the exercise you just completed, your friend's arm represents those little distractions of daily life, the thoughts that spring up to distract you. When you pay as little attention to thoughts of fear, anger, limitation as you did to your friend's arm, you'll be on your way to one-pointed attention.

Every basketball player has experienced the difference between shooting a basket with full attention and attempting the same with only partial concentration. For example, if Stretch is about to shoot, and his attention is divided between the basket and the opponent guard behind him, he's likely to miss a shot he could do easily in practice.

Here's a basketball exercise for you.

▷ ——————————————————————————

Trash-basket Ball: Sit about 10 feet away from a wastebasket. Crumple some paper into about twenty little balls. Get ready to play.

Step 1. Without paying real attention, casually toss some balls toward the basket, and see if any sink in.

Step 2. This time, focus your attention intently by staring in the *center* of the wastebasket. Sink your mind into the basket. Staying relaxed, toss a few balls in. (Remember not to "try" or you'll tense; just let them go in.) Check your results. Were you focused?

Step 3. Do the same as step 2, but once in a while, at random, have a friend standing behind you poke you in the ribs as you're about to shoot. Notice what that does to mental focus and your accuracy.

You may discover that your concentration and attention follow your eyes. One-pointed attention corresponds to intense eye focus. What "Keep your eye on the ball" really means is "Keep your *mind* on the ball."

Developing one-pointed attention, and thus gaining freedom from internal distractions and problems, will help you to master any game. In addition, the mental powers you develop will have tremendous carry-over benefits in the Game of Life. As you stabilize your ability to focus attention fully on the matter at hand, you find yourself resting more and more in the present moment. Free of internal complications, your daily life itself will become more simple, more direct, more profound and full.

The potential for mental training through a natural whole-body approach to training demonstrates how athletics can be a complete educational process. But what I want to emphasize is, all this doesn't take place automatically. If training is not fully conscious or systematic, then mental qualities are only developed randomly and haphazardly. You must be able to *isolate* mental qualities before you can develop them.

For example, if you felt something wrong with your running as you loped around a track—but weren't able to pinpoint the specific problem—you would probably just continue with your physical training, striving to improve through more practice. However, if you were able to identify the specific problem—that your shoes were on the wrong feet—you could immediately take steps to correct the situation.

Many golfers go through periods where they just can't seem to sink a putt. Tennis players have "double-fault slumps." These frustrated athletes may look to the heavens, wondering why the gods are punishing them; they may start carrying rabbit's feet wrapped in garlands of four-leaf clovers; they may develop nervous tics, or voluntarily commit themselves to rest homes—because they can't identify the source of their problem.

Now that you have a better understanding of the mental structures and mechanisms that influence your game, you don't ever need to become stuck for long in that kind of a slump. You can take conscious control of your mental status by straightening out any problems in daily life which may be distracting you—then sink those putts and really fire those serves.

There is no such thing as body-mind harmony. The body doesn't naturally harmonize with the contents of the mind.

Only *no-mind* (or no thought) can naturally harmonize with the body. With mind clear, the body is at its peak efficiency and awareness.

The brain is, of course, useful for a conceptual understanding of your sport, and in analyzing the fundamentals of movement. During the moments of action, however, thinking-feeling processes should be stilled. If mind and body are both active during action, it's like two outfielders running for the same fly ball, yelling, "I've got it! I've got it!" When you are in action, it's best to "lose your mind, and come to your senses."

You've now seen how the mind, dissolved in pure attention, can become focused awareness. You can appreciate the mind's profound influence on movement. Now you are developing a map of understanding. Next, we look to the emotions, which furnish the *fuel* for your journey.

5 EMOTIONAL TALENT

Fueling the fires

If your body is ill, feeble—even bedridden—it will lack vital energy. The muscles will feel drained. Yet there's another kind of energy that can still be burning strong. Its source is the emotional center. This emotional energy we call *motivation*. E-*motion* is what moves us. As you'll see, when the emotions are open and free of obstructions, motivational energy is natural to us, remaining strong even when the body is drained. This feeling energy is what carries the marathon runner past the "wall of pain" when his physical energy reserves are exhausted. On the other hand, a strapping athlete may burst with vital physical energy, but lack the impulse to get moving, because his motivational energy (found in the heart center) is blocked.

On any journey—whether through the world of athletics or through daily life—you must have the energy of motivation in order to move, improve, and succeed. You may completely understand the journey; but without action, nothing happens. Without motivation, you wouldn't get out of bed in the morning . . . ever again.

Motivation *is* emotional talent. It's the key to training. Once released, it can work wonders. It smothers fear; it steamrolls over obstacles. I've seen athletes for whom I would never have predicted success develop into national-caliber champions because of motivation.

One young man whom I'll call Eric had none of the necessary suppleness required for the sport of gymnastics. He moved like a dinosaur. One time in the shower room, some practical joker turned off the cold-water spigot, so only the steaming hot water began spraying down on Eric's back. He seemed to sniff the air, as if he smelled something burning . . . then, with an "*Aaah!*" he lumbered out of the spray. Through sheer work, through countless repetitions of routines, over and over and over, Eric began to move a little faster, a little easier. He transformed himself into one of the nation's top all-around gymnasts.

Another teammate of mine whom I'll call John had polio as a child. His legs were so atrophied that when I first saw him, he had to walk with braces or on crutches. He became a specialist on men's still rings. He simply worked harder than anyone. It wasn't enough to develop superior strength. He also began to practice a dismount from the rings which flew about nine feet in the air. He performed a full-twisting somersault and by some incredible feat of will, landed unassisted on those spindly legs. Over and over I'd see him crash to the floor. His brother told me he used to go home and cry, the pain in his legs was so intense. After three years, John was able to run around the gym with the team without leg braces . . . and he placed second in the national championships. John and Eric had burning motivation.

In daily life, little tasks that require only a modest amount of energy do not require great motivation for their completion. The world of athletics, however, demands much more of a man or woman. Becoming a natural, whole-body athlete demands everything you have within you. Therefore, this path requires tremendous motivational energy.

Most of us relate to motivation passively, as if it were something that descended upon us, outside our control. One day we may say, "I feel motivated today," and the very next day, "I'm just not motivated." The message of this chapter is this: All the motivational energy you'll ever need is within you. *Emotional talent* is the capacity to stimulate and draw upon your natural fountain of energy. Developing emotional talent is learning to blow into your own sails.

Just as we examined the mechanisms of the mind in order to transcend them, we can achieve insight into old emotional habits which block our natural desire to learn.

The anger, fear, and sorrow that we call emotions are not true emotion at all—they are actually *obstructions* to the flow of natural energy. To understand this better, let's look back to our infancy:

When we were babies, motivation was natural to us and constant. Everything was interesting to us. On occasion we might have tensed our little bodies and cried, but crying was a simple, natural response to physical discomfort, not complex mental concerns. Our general state was a clear mind and relaxed body. Our mind and body were in their natural relationship—mind, *free of thought*, in a state of clarity, focus, and attention; body, *free of tension*, full of feeling, sensitivity, and vitality. We experienced the state of pure energy—the energy of motivation—psychic fuel for action, a powerful impulse to move, to explore, and to learn.

As we grew older, and more aware of the rules, meanings, and demands of the world, we began to feel a separation from the protected cradle of infancy. Vulnerable to a world of psychic turbulence, social turmoil, and human frustration, we began to know guilt, fear, and anxiety. As our minds became depositories of traumatic memories (unique to each child but common to all), our bodies began to store tension. This tension was most acutely experienced as a cramp in the chest or abdominal region, but also in the lower back, neck, jaws, and so forth.

It is this feeling of tension, which you can observe in yourself today in times of stress, that we normally call emotion. The tension or cramp is only a *blockage* of the natural flow of emotional energy. Because it is blocked, much as water flowing through a hose might be blocked, we feel pressure at the points of psychophysical tension. The energy gathers in knots, taking shape as what we call anger or fear or sorrow, depending upon what thoughts stimulated that tension.

Emotional blocks (or tension) are reactions to thoughts. If you're standing in line at the bank and someone butts in front of you, you may immediately "feel angry." An infant wouldn't become upset by someone butting in line, because he hasn't yet incorporated society's responses to such an action. But you have learned that "people should wait their proper turn in line." Perhaps true enough, socially. Yet it is such meanings that stimulate emotional reactions. Only the mind free of meanings and judgments and expectations can allow the free flow of emotional energies—free of reactions of fear, sorrow, and anger.

Fear, sorrow, and anger are the three primary emotional obstructions—and like the three primary colors they combine to form a wide spectrum of emotional blocks (such as impatience, frustration, melancholy, anxiety, and so forth).

Fear, sorrow, and anger are normal. That is, they are the usual experience of most people in the world today. Therefore, such obstructions cannot be called neurotic unless we're willing to call our entire society neurotic (which is an interesting and by no means unheard-of possibility). Emotional blocks *are* normal; they are the norm in society—but they are not *natural*, or indigenous to us. Infants, as I have said, may cry from physical discomfort, but they are naturally free from the complex mental structures which often result in turmoil and tension. Fear, sorrow, and anger, as they manifest in adult society, are reactive patterns of subconscious learned behavior.

Though this whole issue is certainly open to debate, we cannot deny that reactive tension—which slows reflexes, interferes with mental clarity, and blocks motivation—is maladaptive to effective action and therefore anathema to the athlete. If a growling dog jumps out at you with its teeth bared, it may be appropriate for you to freeze in your steps (and pretend you're a tree), to run (if you can get away), to kick it (if it's a bluffing poodle), or to climb the nearest telephone pole. Any of these natural reactions can be performed immediately without the involuntary reactive tension we interpret as fear. And, in fact, such tension will only serve to delay the appropriate response.

I don't propose that the aspiring athlete (or anyone else) resolve to become a computer, repressing all show of feelings. There are times it is appropriate to express sorrow or anger or even fear. What I do propose is that anyone who aspires to become a *total* athlete at least gain insight into the mind's influence on emotional tension—in order to be free of unconscious and involuntary reactions which block the natural flow of emotional energy we call motivation.

Tension is not useful to the body. Its debilitating effects on blood circulation, muscle response, etc., have been well documented. You can be free of tension if you're willing to let go of your rigid, conditioned points of view and attitudes about what *should be*. In the athletic arena and at home, remain relaxed in body, with breath full and slow, with mind attentive to what's going on around you, without thinking *about* everything.

Breaking the circuit of tension

Once you acknowledge that the mind imposes tension on the body, it may still be almost impossible to rid yourself of worries. So worry if you must. But apply nonresistance. Let the thoughts float by as they will. And learn to use the following exercise to break the harmful circuit of mental stress becoming physical tension. It couldn't be easier. Follow this simple technique, and you'll be more relaxed, healthier, gaining a kind of physical immunity from worry, fear, etc.

▷ **TENSE—SHAKE—BREATHE—RELAX**

• First tense your whole body, every muscle, as tightly as you can for five seconds, while holding your breath.

• Then shake your body, letting shoulders, belly, and arms flop loosely, like rubber. Shake one leg, then the other, like jelly.

• Stand still, feeling tall, as if your head is suspended in space from a string, and breathe slowly and deeply from your lower belly. Breathe very evenly.

• Let the breath bring a sense of deep relaxation with each inhalation. Feel as if you're floating in space.

• Finally, go about your business. If you're among people when you want to make use of this practice, you can forgo the shaking. Just tense, feel loose, breathe, and relax. No one around you will notice—except that more sensitive people standing nearby will begin to "feel good," picking up on your feeling of well-being.

• Extra amounts of vitamins C and B-complex, in addition to this relaxation-release exercise, will help you achieve balance when you are feeling overwhelmed by problems.

It isn't easy undoing habits formed over the years, but you can do it. In any moment, you have the capacity to breathe deeply, relax, and let go. Surrender happily to whatever arises in the present moment. Let it be interesting rather than "good" or "bad." Then you'll reawaken true emotion, the energy to *act* with momentum and power. Then your life will begin to loosen up and flow. "Flow" is the special talent of the total athlete.

You'll recall that in examining the natural law of *accommodation,* you observed that "life develops what it demands." The corollary of that principle says *what is not used becomes obsolete.* For example, on the physical level, if you don't use a muscle, it atrophies—it becomes weak. It's the same for reactive emotional habit patterns; through nonuse, you can make them obsolescent.

Mastery of athletics requires transcendence of any unconscious reactions that may interfere with the smoothest and most harmonious functioning of the body-mind. Therefore, it's supremely useful to begin the practice of *nondramatization* in the face of circumstances that would otherwise tie you up in knots.

Nondramatization consists of immediate recognition of your psychophysical reality, acknowledging any physical or emotional tension you may feel, and then a conscious letting go: Release the tension, breathe slowly and deeply, act positively and effectively. Trust instinct. Feel *good,* mentally and physically, in spite of whatever negative thoughts may be bouncing around in your head. Negative thoughts don't have to mean negative feelings or tension— *if* you are willing to let go of the thoughts; if you are willing to let yourself feel good in breath and body. That is the essence of nondramatization, and that practice, once proficient, will enable you to transcend the usual knee-jerk reflex of unconscious tension in the face of a difficulty.

Acknowledging an emotional obstruction—("I'm afraid," "I feel angry")—can be constructive. But meditating on it, making that block the compulsive center of your

---

speech and action, is another thing altogether. Here is an example:

Let's say you're walking down the street and a situation arises which stimulates a fearful thought. Maybe a snake slithers in your path; maybe a kid with a knife or a big spider heads in your direction. Okay, you have a fearful thought, and you buy it before you realize what's happening. Instantly then, you feel emotional tension—you feel afraid. So far, this is a description of the usual reactive pattern most people experience. *At this point, however, you can short-circuit the usual habit pattern.*

You don't have to bring a thought or its corresponding tension *to life*; you don't have to dramatize it. You may notice a fearful thought; you may feel afraid—but you *don't have to act afraid.* You don't have to hold your head and scream "OHMYGOD!" You do not have to act out the role of someone who is afraid.

Until you've mastered all emotional obstructions (a degree of mastery not many of us are likely to attain), you'll still encounter situations that stimulate fear, anger, or sorrow; but *what you do in response* to those feelings *is* subject to your control. It is not easy to refrain from dramatizing a reactive pattern. When you're angry with someone, you feel *compelled* to let them know in some way, by exploding in anger or by holding it in and withholding positive life energy from them. But the natural athlete can't afford to hang on to compulsive, reactive baggage.

You don't need to surrender to the reactive pattern by dramatizing it. On the other hand, you don't have to try to ignore or resist it; it's not helpful to pretend you don't feel it. But no matter what you *think* you feel, you can learn to translate your responses into positive energy and action and, ultimately, into emotional maturity. Then, over a period of time, as emotional obstructions are left un-dramatized, they'll grow weaker until finally they become obsolete. Even tension that has been stored for years will then begin to dissolve. Without a single stretching exercise, your muscles will become more resilient and responsive. You'll start to experience, more and more, true emotional energy in the form of relaxed motivation. This energy heals chronic dis-ease, and can literally change your body—and its relationship to the world.

In advocating nondramatization, it may seem that I am suggesting a computerlike existence, without life or passion. Let me reiterate that this is not so. I'm simply describing a psychophysical reality that you can make use of on your journey. You must have insight into the true nature of your emotions in order to gain mastery over them.

Many people who seem like passionate individuals are simply exploiting the superficial manifestations of their vitality while living a life of reactive emotions. Such people may be withdrawn one moment and hysterical the next. True passion, like that of the infant, is focused, free, relaxed—full of feeling and unobstructed energy. The natural athlete generates motivation that is loving and compassionate, not merely enthusiastic or hysterical. When you are around such a person, you can feel his passion enlivening you and flowing through you; not just bouncing off you.

Breath and feeling

"Inspiration," in addition to its usual connotation, also means to breathe in. The breath is a key to your emotional state, because it both reflects—and can control—your level of tension. Learning to breathe properly, with full feeling, gives you the ability quite literally to "inspire" yourself. The natural athlete, like the infant, breathes naturally, from deep in the body, with slow, full, relaxed, and balanced inhalations and exhalations.

To understand your emotional state and to gain mastery over emotions, it's essential that you begin to observe and gain conscious control over your breathing. Breath awareness and discipline were central to the teachings of the most ancient spiritual traditions. Yogis, Zen masters, and martial artists have all placed great emphasis on breathing properly.

The one unifying link between mind and body is the breath. Meditation deals with the mind—but could also be called a physical relaxation exercise. Relaxation exercises, in turn, deal with the body—but could also be called meditation exercises. Both body and mind are intimately related to the emotions, through *feeling the breath*. The various approaches to well-being demonstrate the intimate relationship of the three centers. Meditation practices center around insight and release of thought. As thoughts are released, emotions flow naturally, and the body relaxes. Coming from another direction, you can emphasize relaxation of the body. As the body relaxes, the mind tends to become quiet as well, and the emotions open. All the various approaches to well-being are only ways to re-awaken the natural athlete within us.

If you were to observe your breathing for a few hours during the day, you would notice periods of fitful breathing, with starts and stops, holding of the breath, tension in the chest area, limiting the breathing to shallow gulps of air in the upper chest. If you studied your breathing—and that of others over a long period of time— you would see that the three primary emotional obstructions, anger, sorrow, and fear, are each characterized by an imbalance in breathing. Anger is reflected by weak inhalation and forceful, exaggerated exhalation. Sorrow (as in sobbing) is characterized by spasmodic, fitful inhalation, and weak exhalation. Fear can result in very little breathing at all. As you develop awareness of your breathing patterns through conscious intent, you can become responsible for the recognition of reactive patterns as error, and can then use the breath as a key method of balancing body, mind, and emotions.

The following exercise will give you a feeling for proper breathing and its effect on the body:

▷ —————————————————————————

Sit comfortably, either on a chair or on a cushion. The spine should be upright, but not stiff.

Tension breathing. For a few minutes, breathe with the shoulders raised upward; breathe using the upper chest only; take shallow breaths. Experience how this feels.

Natural breathing. Relax the shoulders by lifting and dropping them a few times, until they just hang. Feel their weight. Keep the mouth closed, the chin tucked gently in, and the eyes closed.

Breathe slowly and deeply, but without any sense of strain. When you inhale, feel your belly draw downward and slightly outward. When you exhale, let the belly relax back up and in. Do this for at least ten minutes, remembering to relax the shoulders, to keep the mouth closed, to notice the rise and fall of the belly. Experience what natural breathing feels like.

As natural breathing becomes more natural for you, you can apply it to your athletic play and everyday activities. Soon, your breathing will be more conscious and timed rhythmically to the force and rhythm of your movements, giving them grace and ease. Ultimately, you will feel that your breath moves your body, freeing yourself from unnecessary muscular effort. Whenever you *notice* that you feel tense, just focus your attention on *feeling* the pleasure of slow, deep, relaxed breathing. Let the shoulders hang. In a few moments, you'll feel the change.

Controlling the breath is but one of the areas where we can exercise control over our wild and random emotional reactions. You see that it isn't necessary to passively wait for thoughts to go away or "get better," nor is it necessary to wait for emotions to become snow pure before you stop dramatizing your reactions. All you need to do is to change your action. Speak positively. Act positively, whether or not you feel like it. This requires discipline—but discipline is what we're up to! We change, and our world changes.

6 PHYSICAL TALENT

Building the foundation

As mental clarity lights your path and emotional energy furnishes the fuel, the body becomes the *vehicle* of action. Even if you understand the road and are gassed up, the journey is only possible if the vehicle is in good shape. In the opinion of doctors, exercise physiologists, coaches, and athletes, what constitutes "good shape" has changed over the years.

There was a time when size meant condition. Big men, big chests, big muscles seemed to be positive indicators of strength and therefore fitness. More recently, fitness has been defined in terms of cardiovascular efficiency. It's probable that coming generations will turn to new concepts of fitness, defined perhaps by the nervous system. And as the popular definitions of fitness change, so will the popular fitness activities. We've seen an evolution from the weight lifting of years ago to today's jogging and other aerobic activities; perhaps next the emphasis will be on breathing, yoga, meditation, hot mineral baths, massage, and relaxation techniques.

In outlining how to develop your *physical talent* for movement activities I've included key elements that aren't normally emphasized in the popular literature. Traditional fitness is only part of the picture.

Take a moment—or a lifetime—to appreciate your body. There is no greater miracle in nature. Its complexities fill encyclopedias, and still there's more to be said. The body can contemplate the cosmos over breakfast, write poetry over tea. The body that holds this book is the only one *you'll* ever have—reincarnation or not, *you're* not going to remember—its warranty is limited, good for a short time only. Let's look at the body's care, feeding, and development.

Because the mind and emotions are difficult to observe and can be resistant to change, the body is an ideal medium to work with in developing whole-body talent. The body is a plastic form, which can be reshaped by the intelligent application of energy. Its state reflects—and influences— the nature of the mind and emotions. Therefore, in developing physical talent, you are going to effect corresponding changes in mental and emotional realms. *Conscious physical training is using the visible to mold the invisible.*

Reshaping the body. Natural training is no more and no less than aligning the body's shape and movements to natural forces. For example, look at your body's relationship to gravity.

There are only two stable positions in gravity: horizontal and vertical. If your body is lying flat or standing straight, it's naturally aligned in gravity. However, if the body is out of line—if it has poor posture—then extra energy is required to keep it stable in the pull of gravity. You would need to lean on something or someone, or else exert muscular effort, to maintain your position.

Take a moment to stand up, then lean forward or sideward or backward a few degrees, from the waist. You'll soon feel a pressure or slight tension in the muscles which must now work to hold you up. If you held that position for a minute, two minutes, or more, it would soon become painful, because you're not standing in a natural position in gravity.

▷ GETTING STRAIGHT

For ten minutes, try maintaining excellent, tall, stretched, erect posture, with a long back, chin gently tucked in, back of head stretched upward, with shoulders relaxed. Maintain this whether standing, sitting, or moving. In experiencing how difficult this is (unless you are already naturally aligned), you can appreciate the importance of reshaping the body.

If you're like most of us, your body *is* probably out of line, deviating to some degree from perfect vertical alignment. This misalignment can be a result of childhood accidents, incorrect movement patterns and compensations, occupational or sports imbalances, or even emotional traumas which resulted in stored tensions and shortened muscles.

An aggressive person often holds his head or chin slightly forward, resulting in chronic tension in the neck muscles. If you injured an ankle years ago and began to favor it, you may have caused compensatory reactions up through the knee, hip, and shoulders. Some people have a pattern of holding the belly in or pulling the pelvis back—each causing misalignment in gravity.

These and similar postural imbalances within the force of gravity result in a chronic tension. Energy is wasted, since muscular effort is constantly required to hold the body up. Fatigue sets in too often and too much. (Of course, diet, sleep habits, and other variables can also contribute to fatigue—but postural imbalance is a major source of energy drain.)

Constant physical tension may go unnoticed, since you've become accustomed to it over the years. It results in a chronic sense of discomfort, with constant shifting and fidgeting, nervousness, and even emotional irritability.

Chronic tension and fatigue are reflected in many symptoms, ranging from headaches to lower back pain. The stored tensions produce a hardening of the connective tissue and lowered blood circulation, resulting in limited mobility or stiffness.

In examining the anatomy of physical talent, I've begun with posture, because it expresses the body's relationship to a primary natural force—gravity. It doesn't serve for me to advise you to "relax" until you understand and can become responsible for your alignment with gravity.

There are forms of massage and systems of body manipulation which can aid your conscious efforts to realign your body segments in a more natural pattern in stillness and motion. If your connective tissue has become chronically shortened due to chronic tension, it does little good to try to have good posture, because as soon as you relax, the shortened tissue will pull the body parts into the habitually misaligned position. Therefore, in many cases, some deep body work may be indicated—such as structural integration, popularly called rolfing, or polarity massage, Reichian massage, or other form of deep manipulation of tissue—or, in the case of chiropraxis, manipulation of the axial skeletal system.

The shape of the body can be changed in other ways, too, Conscious exercise can be used to pinpoint weak areas, and to strengthen them. By "conscious exercise," I don't mean random game play—I mean specific supplementary exercises to help balance the body. If you're very strong but lack suppleness, hatha yoga practice will serve to extend your range of motion. On the other hand, if you're a loosey-goosey type, specific strength-building exercises will serve to give you more control and stability. Through well-balanced and regular exercise, your body will naturally respond.

HANGING: BALANCING GRAVITY'S CRUNCH

Without gravity, you'd soon become a mass of mush, without muscle tone, with weak circulation of blood and lymph, totally susceptible to any unusual stresses on the body. The field of gravity is the Great Developer, a twenty-four-hour exercise laboratory. Astronauts must exercise or create artificial gravity.

On the other hand, gravity's pull can also be debilitating. You are being compressed all day; the vertebrae are pressed, one against the other, with only small pads between them, and your feet bear a great burden. Your joints are compressed hour after hour.

The most simple way to balance gravity's crunch is to *hang* every day. In the morning and evening, grab hold of a bar or solid door sill . . . or make a simple hanging bar that will easily support your weight. Hang for ten seconds to half a minute. Feel the joints opening, the spine gently stretching out.

Resistance to change

The body, like the mind and emotions, has a tendency to resist change. It settles into certain movement patterns, and only conscious effort can change these patterns.

Resistance is related to Newton's law of inertia and momentum which states, "A body at rest tends to stay at rest, and a body in motion tends to stay in motion, unless acted upon by an external force." To translate that into the kind of resistance-to-change I'm talking about, we might say, "A body that begins in balance tends to stay in balance, and a body out of balance tends to stay that way too . . . unless acted upon by an outside force."

Your body was in balance, many years ago—until it was acted upon by many forces, both psychological and physical, which, as you've seen by now, generated a variety of imbalances in mind, emotions . . . and body. The outside force which you can generate is the force of your motivations.

If you want to carry the Staff of Realism on your journey, brand the following principle onto your psyche: *Any change requires an initiatory period of discomfort, until the body adjusts to the new demand.* You will experience this discomfort as you develop your talent; there is no way of getting around it. You'll feel the discomfort as symptoms, ranging from tiredness when you begin a new exercise program to various psychophysical tensions and pain as you stop old habits. The "pain" may be mild in some cases—for example, if you streamline your diet, you'll feel hunger pangs or cravings. The pain can be more severe—as when you stop a drug habit. But all these symptoms are only signs of the body readjusting, and they will pass.

In changing to a new pattern of diet or exercise or life habits, you'll find the initiatory period of discomfort lasting three to four weeks. By the end of that time, you'll have adapted to your new pattern. However, the period of *stabilization* takes from three to six months. During this period, your motivation to change must remain strong, because the body will still tend to return to old patterns. That means the dieter will still tend to gain back the weight by returning to the old patterns; the smoker will still develop new cravings if he lights up. Any change in life habits will tend to collapse into the archaic pattern—unless maintained for the period of stabilization. Be patient and persistent then, because it takes time for old patterns to become obsolete.

The laws of accommodation, balance, and natural order all point to the obvious: You absolutely *can* reshape your life patterns and your body through insight, direction, and energy. When mind and motivation work in harmony, what is created is real *will*. If you *see* what must be done, then you simply . . . must . . . *do it*. The real journey, you see, is a journey within your own body.

Feeding the body

Your body is "fed" on many levels—through sunlight and fresh air, peaceful environments, and through affection and energy from friends and family . . . as well as through the food you eat. All these factors are equally important for you to thrive as a complete human being—but the most visible need is to be fed through the intake, digestion, and assimilation of food. The food you eat has a great influence on the shape, function, and overall talent of the body.

How you eat is as important as *what* you eat. The complete cycle of nourishment begins when food is taken in, and continues with its digestion, distribution to where it's needed, utilization of the nutrients, and elimination of toxic wastes. Any weakness in this complete cycle can fundamentally affect your well-being. Therefore, emotional calm, proper eating habits, and appropriate time and place to eat are as important to consider as the food itself. You're wise then to give attention to improving every aspect of the food cycle. That doesn't mean you have to become a nutritional genius. Even little babies, whose instincts are intact, will choose the proper combination of foods for proper nutrition if offered a variety.

I've studied nutrition both from a scientific, academic perspective and from an intuitive, experiential, "health nut" approach. Although I do not intend to tell you what to think or how to eat, I do want to outline what I feel is a natural approach to diet, because it seems best for the natural athlete.

Precivilized man simply ate whatever foods were in season, when they were fresh, without chemical additives, preservatives, or commercial processing. The processing, preserving, coloring, sweetening, and instantizing that characterize many foods today are commercial practices designed to make higher profits by preventing spoilage and loss, and also to attract buyers who are accustomed to bright colors and bland taste and extra sweetness. Whether all this processing adds or detracts from the quality of the food is something you'll have to decide for yourself, as your instincts sharpen. It has become obvious to me. My feeling is, preservatives don't preserve *you*. It stands to reason that if you have, for example, a choice between a yogurt brand with five additives and one with just plain old yogurt, it's wiser to choose the most natural brand.

The reason so many of us need reshaping in the first place is because we tend to eat *too much of what we don't need, and not enough of what we do need*. Most of us tend to eat for "taste treats," using food as a consolation when we're upset or bored. An infant would never do this; neither would your cat—and neither will the natural athlete. As a matter of fact, you may eat things your cat wouldn't *dream* of touching!

If you begin to pay conscious attention—which involves being open, aware, free of self-judgment—you will start to simplify your diet. As you simplify your diet, begin to cut down on between-meal eating, and at least moderate your use of artificially produced products, you will be making important strides toward resensitizing your body. As your body becomes more sensitive, you won't need experts to tell you what you should eat. You'll *know*—you'll feel it. You'll begin to want to eat just what you need—instead of needing to eat just what you want.

No one can escape the operations of natural law. If you eat healthful food, full of its original nutritional value and free from man's additives, and if you eat properly, that food will contribute toward stable and vibrant health. If you eat too much or too little—if you eat insufficient nutrients—there will be an inevitable price to pay. It may not be today or even tomorrow, but you *will* eventually reap the results of your dietary habits.

It isn't easy to eat well in a mass society. It isn't convenient. It takes more time to shop. Therefore, you first have to see *very* realistically how your food can affect your life. Then you will have the motivational momentum to overcome self-indulgent inertia. "You are what you eat." How many times have we heard that old cliché! If it were literally true, we'd see a lot of Twinkies and Hostess Cupcakes walking around. But there is some truth to the old cliché after all.

Diet is nothing more than a matter of simple, ordinary, natural habits of eating. It doesn't require exotic programs or foods. Persistent, natural patterns of diet are the key, not puritan perfectionism; patterns which reflect the body's essential needs rather than the mind's cravings.

Read all the books you want, but knowledge is not a sufficient answer. You must sensitize yourself over a period of time. Really pay attention to what you put into your mouth, and how you feel afterward. Following a natural diet implies that you *act* upon your understanding. Babies "know nothing," yet will eat naturally. Many scientists' bodies reflect the impotence of mere knowledge.

Posture, nutrition, breathing habits, and sleep all must

be balanced according to the natural principles if you are to fill the body with vitality. This vitality, in turn, gives you power to develop your physical talent.

Relaxation is the best single indicator of your whole-body well-being. Your degree of relaxation across the three centers precisely reflects your trust in and alignment with the natural laws. Physical ease is a mirror of the relationship of body to mind. When you are truly relaxed, centered, at ease, the mind comes to rest, the emotions flow clearly, and the vital body surrenders itself to nature's flow. All feels right with the world then, because all feels right with the body.

Like a child, the natural athlete is free from all inhibiting tension. He's come to recognize his tension and learned to release it in the same moment. Thus, he experiences a deep storehouse of energy, sufficient to enjoy a simple life, as well as to bounce through his athletic exploits.

Most of us have carried subtle tensions for so many years, we've forgotten what *real* relaxation is. The moments we come closest to full muscular release is when we're momentarily emptied of tension—after sexual orgasm or a long run or a hot-tub soak or a hard game. Games and fitness activities have become for us ways of throwing off energy, so for a few pleasant hours we feel pleasantly drained.

Genuine relaxation, however, is not a temporary state achieved by dissipating knotted energy; it is a *continual* enjoyment of muscular release *and* high energy at the same time.

All the good advice in the world to "relax" is without value unless you know what it feels like to consciously release habitual muscular tension. You need a *baseline of relaxation* in order to notice those little pockets of tension. The relaxation exercise that follows will serve that purpose. Take the time to *do* this exercise; the benefits are well worth the time and attention you give to it. Just imagining "what the exercise must be like" isn't going to be useful.

▷ ─────────────────────────────────────

Begin by lying on your back on a carpet or mattress, and loosen any tight clothing. Have a friend read the instructions, or record them and play them back. Once you know the steps, you can repeat them silently to yourself:

"Be aware of the body's weight. Breathing slowly and naturally, surrender to gravity. Notice the floor pressing up against the body, and the body pressing equally down into the floor.

"Put your attention on your feet . . . imagine that they are very heavy. Feel the skin heavy, the bones heavy . . . the whole body becoming heavy. . . .

"Feel the deep, profound heaviness spreading up into your lower legs and through the knees, releasing all the muscles. Feel the lower legs heavy . . . the skin heavy, the bones heavy . . . the whole body becoming heavy.

"Feel the heaviness continue into the thighs and buttocks. Feel all the muscles of the thighs release, and the buttocks relax. Feel the skin heavy, the bones heavy . . . the whole body becoming heavy.

"Release all the muscles around the abdomen and chest, as the breath continues effortlessly. Feel the skin heavy, the bones heavy . . . the whole body becoming heavy.

"Let the pleasant heaviness sink deep into the lower back, releasing . . . and continue into the upper back, around and under the shoulder blades, along the spine . . . releasing . . . heavy. Let the muscles of the upper back and neck and shoulders sink into gravity's pull . . . skin heavy, bones heavy . . . the whole body heavy.

"Let go of the upper arms . . . the elbows and lower arms . . . feel the heaviness all the way to the fingertips . . . skin, bones . . . the whole body . . . heavy.

"Feel all the muscles of the neck . . . front, back, and sides, release and sink to the floor . . . skin, bones . . . the whole body heavy.

"Now the entire body below the neck is heavy, totally relaxed. If you feel any tension left anywhere, let it go, and become twice as heavy.

"Now, as I name the areas of the face and scalp, feel them as heavy, and let them go with gravity . . . skin, bones . . . the whole body . . . heavy . . .

"Feel the scalp release . . . all the muscles of the forehead . . . around the eye sockets . . . the cheeks, letting go . . . the muscles around the nose . . . the mouth and jaw, all releasing . . . the chin, and around the ears.

─────────────────────────────────────

"Now your entire body is in deep relaxation. Energies flow through the body freely, revitalizing, healing, rebalancing.

"Notice the breathing. Imagine you're floating gently, on your own warm, private ocean. On inhalation, feel yourself float slowly up, and on exhalation, float back down . . . feeling the well-being of total relaxation.

"Imagine the blood coursing freely through the body, nourishing it. Feel the energy of the body, vibrating within the cells.

"Feel the peacefulness of relaxation. Notice how calm the mind is in this moment—and how open the emotional feelings are. The next time you experience any emotional upset, let the body relax into this pleasant state.

"Imagine yourself walking, with this same feeling of release . . . using only the muscular effort you need, and no more. Feel the lightness and effortlessness of running . . . or playing your favorite sport with the same relaxed grace. . . .

"As you feel this state, know that you can return to it at will. Now begin to increase the depth of your breathing. Ending with three gigantic breaths of energy, open your eyes, and sit up. Stretch like a cat."

Studies of efficiency in movement, carried out at several universities, showed that people tend to use wasted effort and unnecessary muscular tension in even the simplest movements—lifting a fork, holding a book, sitting in a chair. Not only did the subjects use more tension than necessary; they also tensed muscles that were unrelated to the movements being made.

As you become acclimated to deep relaxation, you'll naturally begin to notice more and more the tension you have carried unconsciously. Now it will become conscious and therefore under your control. If you remember to relax whenever you notice tension—and if you notice tension more and more—you'll have made a giant step on the path of the natural athlete.

TESTING FOR RELAXATION

Ask a friend to lift your arm as you endeavor to let it hang limp. Notice whether or not you unconsciously "help" your friend lift your arm, or whether the arm is totally dead weight. Do this experiment with a friend . . . and you'll notice how some people, try as they might, cannot let their arms relax due to chronic, unconscious, and energy-wasting tension they carry with them all day.

As you learn to master this "letting go," it will help you maintain a sense of release throughout the day—and when you do become tense, you'll notice it more readily and can release the tension (TENSE—SHAKE—BREATHE—RELAX).

A relaxed arm should shake like jelly when someone takes your hand in both of his hands and shakes vigorously. If your arm is lifted and released, it should drop to your side instantly. If you carry a lot of tension (as do many older people, having stored it over the years), the arm may even stay in place for a long moment before dropping.

The consummate athletes and artists in every field have attained an ease of movement through efficient use of muscles. They waste no effort whether singing, stroking a violin, swinging a tennis racket, or swimming a channel. Relaxation-in-movement is the foundation of physical talent.

The following four main sections, which I call the "Four S's of Talent: Strength, Suppleness, Sensitivity, and Stamina," are really only a postscript to relaxation, as you will see. However, these four attributes encompass the entire range of talent which you can develop for any sport or movement activity.

Strength

If you had no voluntary muscle tissue, you'd spend your very brief life as a puddle of protoplasm, a heap of skin, organs, and bones. People with muscular disabilities appreciate that which we take for granted—the ability to *move at will*.

Now, any physiologist will tell you that if you stimulate enough muscle fibers for a given demand over a period of time, the body will create larger fibers to meet the demand. The muscular strength increases in proportion to the effort of training. That all seems straightforward. Yet there's more to muscle than meets the eye.

Anyone knows that strength is one of the primary qualities of physical talent. What many of us may not have considered, however, is how to *use* strength properly in balance with relaxation. "Strength" is more than the ability to contract muscle tissue; strength is the overall ability to *control movement.*

A teammate of mine at the University of California could easily press himself up to a handstand from a prone position—flat on his belly on the floor. (To appreciate this, you might lie down on your belly and imagine just bending your arms as if to do a push-up, but trying to push your entire body right up to a handstand.) Brad was obviously well-muscled.

In order to accomplish this movement, Brad primarily used triceps (extensor or pushing) muscles, as well as deltoid (shoulder) muscles. He could accomplish this movement over and over in practice. In competition, however, when he usually became tense, he unconsciously tightened too many muscles. Instead of just using his extensor muscles, he also tensed his biceps (flexor or pulling) muscles. Thus, his antagonistic muscle groups "fought" one another, resulting in a standoff and exhaustion. He couldn't push up.

In order to be effectively strong in competition, he had to practice relaxation of unnecessary muscles. In the same way, many athletes who train intensively for strength, developing large, powerful muscles, may nevertheless have diminished *effective strength* because they are generally tense, and haven't "educated" their appropriate muscle groups in complementary tension-relaxation. Thus, they can't run as fast, leap as high, or react as quickly.

Effective strength is the ability to relax the proper muscle groups while consciously tensing others. It may come as no surprise to you that babies do this naturally. Put your finger in a baby's grasp, and try to pull away. Those little hands are surprisingly strong. They demonstrate relaxed power.

One study compared the movement abilities of six-month-old babies and some professional athletes. The athletes tried to copy every movement and posture of these babies . . . for ten minutes. Not a single athlete could keep up. They all dropped out from exhaustion within a few minutes.

Men may develop great bulk and perform feats of brute strength, as in weight lifting, but in lightness, speed, and most economic use of strength, it may be the women athletes who will shine, because they tend to develop less muscular tension. The young women gymnasts are excellent examples of effective strength in action. And look at the cat! You won't see any muscle-bound cats walking around, yet what athlete can match a cat's movement abilities? I've seen cats jump ten feet straight up to a roof from a sitting position. A cat can be napping, then instantly spring after a mouse with blinding speed, then, just as suddenly, stop and clean its paws, totally relaxed. The cat carries very little tension. You can squeeze its muscle to the bone, and it will show no pain. Try squeezing your calf muscles to the bone, and feel the accumulated tension.

Various exercise systems emphasize relaxation-in-movement as a primary objective. One system taught by Arica Institute, called eurythms, entails the gradual tensing and relaxing of different parts of the body to a regular rhythm while maintaining complete relaxation elsewhere. Eventually it's possible to master the conscious tensing of twelve different parts of the body independently. Training like this is very useful before running out and pumping iron.

As in the other sections, I am not outlining many individual *how to* exercises, because although you can learn *about* movement from a book, it is immensely difficult and usually inappropriate to learn *how to* move from a book. Everyone has individual needs. It's best to get individual feedback from a teacher.

However, there are a few simple routines you can perform to experience relaxed strength. The first comes from the flowing martial art of aikido. This exercise is done with a partner, who will gradually try to bend your arm twice—the first time against your resistance, the second time against your *nonresistance*.

Test 1. Hold your right arm out in front of you, fist clenched, arm *slightly* bent, with your wrist on your partner's shoulder. Your partner puts one hand on the crook of your elbow and gradually begins to push down, in order to bend your arm (in the direction it normally bends, of course). You resist, tensing your arm.

Shake your arm loose, and begin.

Test 2. Standing balanced, place your wrist on your partner's shoulder as before—this time, with your fingers extended and spread.

Your partner will again begin pushing gradually downward as if to bend your arm.

This time, however, you'll remain free of tension. Let your arm be totally relaxed, yet strong—not like a wet noodle. You do this by imagining a powerful flow of energy, like water gushing through a hose, continually flowing through your arm and out the ends of your extended fingers, shooting right through the wall for a thousand miles.

Let your awareness "flow" with the energy and not stop at your partner's hands. Keep your intent focused on maintaining an extended (but not locked) arm. As your partner begins to push more, imagine an increase in the power of the flow, balancing his pressure.

Experiment with this, and see if you begin to feel a new kind of strength, free of tension.

For those accustomed to this kind of strength, the arm becomes nearly unbendable when relaxed and actually much "weaker" when tensed. It doesn't work because of a magical energy flow, but because you are using only the amount of muscle tissue you actually need. This develops not only great effective strength, but a feeling of ease.

Now if you like, you can do another simple exercise that highlights how mental attitude can influence effective strength.

▷ ————————————————————————————————
In this exercise, you will do two push-ups with tension and two free of tension.

1. Beginning from an up position, do 2 push-ups at a slow-to-moderate pace, with *every* muscle in your body *tensed.* This is what it's like to *try.* Clench your teeth, tighten your thighs, buttocks, stomach, neck . . . it's exhausting, and makes the push-ups seem difficult, right?
    To a lesser extent, this is what most athletes do during training, since few athletes have practiced conscious relaxation-in-movement.

2. For the second 2 push-ups, imagine that you're a puppet on a string, suspended from the arms of a giant who is standing directly over you. The giant will do the work for you. Starting from the same up position, just relax down effortlessly, and imagine the giant quickly pulling you up on the strings. Let the push-up happen by itself.

By sustaining and acting upon the image of energy flow or a movement happening by itself, you create the psycho-physical effect of relaxed strength—and all three centers tend to harmonize in their natural relationship.

Strength cannot be free to work unless balanced with relaxation. The height you can jump from a stand is a factor of both your ability to relax, and *then* to push and spring. Try standing up, crouching down a bit, tensing your legs as hard as you can . . . then jumping. You can hardly move.

Dale was captain of the Stanford gymnastics team. He was a floor-exercise and tumbling specialist. He was one of the hardest workers on the team. Each day, Dale would begin with calisthenics, squat jumps for leg strength; he ran about three miles every day; he practiced his tumbling sequences over and over and over. His legs were well-muscled and his diet excellent. He was slim, yet his tumbling made him look as though he weighed 500 pounds; he just couldn't seem to get up into the air. A few beginning tumblers with legs like toothpicks would run out and tumble higher than he could. It used to drive him crazy.

Dale had developed too much muscle and too much tension. Muscle weighs more than fat. As muscle bulk and weight triples, strength only doubles. There is a point, especially for someone who must *move his own body* rapidly and lightly, where development becomes over-development. Dale could have spent an entire summer without a single strength drill, and just practiced relaxation—in order to get stronger. His tumbling would have made a sudden improvement.

Through accommodation, your muscles will develop in response to a demand. Balance that demand between sheer power and the ability to be loose and relaxed. That way, you'll develop full *use* of your muscles, not just "full power."

Once you develop your capacity for *relaxed power*, your movements will take on a new quality of effortlessness and grace, leading to improved speed, coordination, reflexes, and real response-ability—in the gym, on the field, and throughout daily life.

Suppleness

To most of us, suppleness implies stretching exercises. This may be true for the most part. Yet a baby needs no stretching exercises, because it carries no tension—and neither did you, a long time ago. As you grew, however, you began to activate habitual tensing of muscles in response to physical pain, psychological threat, or emotional upset. You began to store unresolved upsets over the years, in the form of tension (just as the body stores nonutilized energy in the form of fat). Therefore, your body became less naturally supple, and remedial exercises like stretching have become necessary.

Tension—leading to stiff joints, aches and pains, and decreased circulation, as well as contributing to arthritic conditions—is an unconscious, maladaptive strategy that we all have to become responsible for. That means noticing our stored tension and using appropriate measures to dissolve it.

The naturally supple body is a reflection of a relaxed mind. However, I'm not suggesting that you start psychoanalysis to undo all past trauma in order to find some peace and flexibility. Just remember to notice tension in the course of your daily life—perhaps in the thighs, neck, back, face, or guts. Notice when you begin to tense, and then relax. Do this more and more. You may never be inclined to invest large amounts of time and energy researching the causes of all those childhood upsets, but you *can* be responsible for tension *in this moment.*

Yes, stretching *is* a remedial activity—but a remedial activity that most of us need. Once you recognize that mental and emotional tension imposed upon the body is the source of your relative degree of stiffness, you can naturally form the right approach to stretching. You can avoid the usual approach of needlessly inflicting even more pain and tension on yourself by improper stretching, by pushing (and pulling) too hard.

Stretching should be relaxed and intelligent—not just enthusiastic.

The usual athlete may push and pull his body through various extended positions either casually or aggressively, gritting his teeth in pain. The rest of the day he only tenses up again, and must repeat the same painful process. He'll probably feel some progress as the body adapts to the daily stretching, but this kind of program is a "two steps forward, one step back" approach. It's painful, and sets up non-pleasurable psychological reactions.

The best recipe I know for suppleness is three parts relaxation to one part stretching. Without doing *any* stretching, you become more supple when you're relaxed, on vacation, or free from usual concerns. (On the other hand, many athletes become tighter, even while stretching, during exam times.)

If you "ask" your body to grow more supple, it will—*if* you ask it *nicely*. The following guidelines are "nice" ways to ask your body to stretch. Make a gentle demand, and you'll receive a positive response.

▷ WHOLE BODY STRETCH

1. You are a stretching expert. You don't need to be seeking the advice of others. You know more about precisely where, and to what degree, you need to stretch than any expert, for the body in question is *yours.*

Simply relax into a slightly more extended position than you're used to, whenever you feel tight. That sounds almost too simple, but that's all there is to it. You don't need to know anatomy. Just feel where you're tense—maybe it's the neck or lower back or behind the knees. If so, gently sit or bend just a little more. *Breathe deeply,* and imagine the breath going to the tight area, relaxing it.

Even you great athletic types should be as gentle with your bodies as if you were 98 years old.

2. Stretching should feel *good*, like a cat stretching after a nap. Balance between pleasure and pain.

3. Stretch only a little, but do it at least twice each day. It's better doing 3 or 4 minutes of relaxed stretching twice a day than 15 minutes of grinding it out, once a day. Sneak up on it; remember to ask the body nicely . . . but ask it often.

4. Stretch when the body is warm. It's easier, it feels better, and it does you

more good when you're warm. (Cold stretching hurts more, and you're more likely to be tense.)

5. Stretch any way you feel like it. I don't normally recommend bouncing vigorously, but a gentle pulsing bounce is okay if that feels good to you. However if you sink into the stretch position for a few deep, relaxed, feel-good breaths, that may allow you to gain more benefits. *Experiment.*

6. Experimentation is the key. Find the most gentle, *pleasurable* way to stretch; it's only another of the body's games, after all. Later, you can develop more challenging stretches.

For the same reason that I don't give any *how to* strength exercises, I won't prescribe any stretching exercises here. Books on hatha yoga offer a good approach. *The Weekend Athlete's Way to a Pain-Free Monday* by H. Jampol is also useful. Even better, you may find a beginning class in hatha yoga, t'ai chi, aikido, dance, or gymnastics useful.

The main thing is for you to determine the suppleness factors that are helpful in your own activity. What movements do you normally make? Where would an extended range of motion help? Gradually make a demand to extend that range of motion.

Suppleness means a state of full articulation of all movable joints, including wrists, shoulders, neck, the entire spine, pelvis, hips, thighs, hamstrings, and ankles. The object of stretching is to open and free all joints, depending upon the demands of your favorite activities. If you become supple beyond the actual point of need, you'll feel an ease of movement. You'll also extend your range of power.

In general, suppleness should be given priority over strength—or at least developed prior to the major strength development—since the more supple you are, the less energy you need to expend in order to move the body. *Suppleness is the embodiment of nonresistance.*

I'm going to mention one important area and how to stretch

---

it properly, because it's a source of pain for beginners in hatha yoga, gymnastics, dance, many sports, and daily life.

If you bend a wire back and forth, it's going to break at the weakest point—the point of major bend. When people bend forward at the waist, the weakest point is the lower back. It's a repository of tension and smack-dab in the point of major pressure. Even bending forward at the waist a few degrees puts tremendous pressure on the lower back. (That's why it is *so* important to lift heavy objects by bending at the knees, keeping the back vertical, and using leg strength to lift.)

The strain on the lower back is multiplied when the hamstring muscles, behind the knees, are tight. The hamstrings are in a stronger position than the muscles of the lower back, relative to forward bending motions, so if both are stiff, it's the lower back that gets sore . . . or worse. Therefore, when bending forward or stretching, it's important for you first to spend time lengthening and strengthening the hamstring area *without* involving the lower back. Don't just sit with legs straight and throw yourself forward to try to grab your toes.

$\triangleright$ HAMSTRING STRETCH
_____

The proper way to stretch the hamstrings is to lie on your back and lift one straight leg up toward a vertical position, with the other leg bent and the foot resting flat on the floor. Gradually, bring the straight leg up to the vertical (or even past vertical) toward your chest. Make sure your lower back remains flat on the floor; don't let it do the work. This takes time to develop, so don't rush. You may wish to use a towel, which you hold in both hands, one on each end, and the towel hooked over the foot of the straight leg.

Remember to keep the straight leg *straight*. Sacrifice elevation for straightness. (Proper position in stretching is as important as proper position in strength development.) You can always determine what the proper position is by how it feels.

For an extra stretch, you can flex your foot (flattening it and curling the toes back toward your head). Once the hamstrings are more supple, any forward stretching or bending motion will be easier on the back.

_____

Suppleness, strength, and relaxation are intimately related. Movement requires all three if it is to become natural. If a joint is frozen, no amount of strength will move it. If you want to lift your leg high into the air to do a dance step, kick a football, or perform a gymnastics movement, you need both strength (to lift the leg) and suppleness (to allow the full range of motion through which the muscles work). Effective movement always requires the integration and balance of suppleness and strength.

Suppleness—developed through awareness of tension, conscious relaxation, and proper stretching—will improve your game and decrease muscle pulls, sprains, and related injuries. It will increase the muscle's responsiveness through increased blood flow. You'll feel more awake and alive in daily life as your range of movement increases. You'll literally feel younger again. You can be as supple as a gymnast or dancer.

If you relax, you'll become supple. As you increase your suppleness, you'll also tend to become more naturally relaxed. In your relaxation, you'll begin to notice another change—and that change is our next topic.

Sensitivity

There was a legendary master of t'ai chi who was so sensitive to the forces around him that if a fly landed on his shoulder, he would sway gently, under its "impact." A sparrow was unable to jump from his open palm and fly, because as it pushed away, his hand would sink beneath its legs. We all enjoy hearing stories about such people, who seem to possess "supernatural" attributes or abilities. Yet the description of this t'ai chi master only reflects natural abilities, refined to a high degree through practice.

Sensitivity just means enhancement of senses, and can

refer to sight, hearing, taste, and so on. Most relevant for the athlete are the proprioceptive and kinesthetic senses which enable him to move effectively. These senses include the following: *balance*, the vertical reflex, or ability to detect subtle divergence from the vertical, and to correct for it; *coordination*, the ability to move different parts of the body independently, with different degrees of muscular contraction, or to unify deliberately all the parts around a central axis of movement; *timing* and *rhythm*, the ability to start or stop a given movement at the correct moment; and *reflex speed*, the ability to respond quickly to a given stimulus.

You might expect someone with excellent coordination to have good timing and rhythm also, superior balance, and fast reflexes. And you would be right. Balance, coordination, timing, rhythm, and reflex speed are all interrelated; they are only different manifestations of neuromuscular *sensitivity*. As you develop greater sensitivity, *many* attributes will shine.

If you concentrate on one area of sensitivity, such as balance, the other areas will also develop. This is one reason it's wise to expose yourself to a variety of movement activities. The proficient tennis player who, in order to improve his *tennis*, takes a beginning gymnastics or dance or hatha yoga class (which place greater demand on the refinements of balance, suppleness, and relaxation) is a wise athlete.

Beyond what has already been outlined, you don't have to *do* anything to achieve greater sensitivity. It's a matter of recognizing tension and relaxing; it's a natural result of stretching gently, of "asking nicely" for greater range of motion each day; it will follow as you develop relaxed strength.

Sensitivity enables you to learn more rapidly and with greater ease, because your body picks up cues faster. You can feel errors more quickly, and correct them with greater consistency. You can copy the experts better, because you open the circuits between your eyes and your muscular feedback. You can cut through old, maladaptive compensations more easily, because you won't be as deeply locked into patterns of tension.

You've learned that you first have to recognize an error before you can correct it. Try this experiment:

▷ ————————————————————————

Look around you and find two objects nearby of different weight. (I used a bottle of suntan lotion and a pencil.)

What you're going to do is pick up one object and put it down, then pick up the other object and put it down—sensing the difference in weight.

Test 1. Before picking up either object, tense your arm as *hard as you possibly can.* Tense the upper arm, the shoulder, the wrist, and the fingers. As you grasp the object, squeeze it tightly before lifting.

Now lift one object, then the other as you tense. Did you notice that it was difficult or impossible to feel the difference in weight?

Test 2. Pick the objects up, one after the other, but let your arm be relaxed. See how easy it is to sense the difference in weight.

There are a number of reasons why you were able to sense the weight difference of the two objects more easily when relaxed, but that isn't important here. The main purpose of the exercise is to show how tension can limit your sensitivity. On more subtle levels, even a small amount of tension interferes with a refined sense of balance, timing, coordination, and reflex speed. The natural athlete is a paragon of apparent contrasts, capable of unleashing awesome power, yet so soft, smooth, and sensitive that he can pick up on the most subtle cues. As your natural training progresses, you'll dissolve even the subtle blocks to learning.

The primary message of this section so far is that it takes more than running out and playing blindly to develop a foundation of natural physical talent. First a natural order of training must be reestablished, with intelligent priorities. That's why I emphasize relaxation above all else. Then it's possible to develop strength properly without waste of energy. Free of unnecessary tension, you can develop suppleness more effectively. All these attributes serve as a foundation of sensitivity, and everything else falls into place.

Nevertheless, learning skills requires practice, and practice requires stamina. We now turn to stamina, and its role in physical talent.

Stamina

The most proficient athletes spend a lot of time playing and practicing. No athlete ever became an expert without investing time and energy. Thus, in its own way, stamina—or the ability to work over a period of time—is a vital aspect of physical talent.

Stamina is a perfect reflection of the law of accommodation—that a demand over a period of time creates a specific development. It takes stamina to perform any action over an extended period of time. Writing a book, for example, requires one kind of stamina, different from running a marathon. Anyone caught in rush-hour traffic or long lines at the bank knows that there are mental and emotional kinds of stamina, too. Since this section deals with physical talent, however, we will focus on physical stamina or endurance.

If you place a demand on your lungs and heart to bring oxygen to the tissues more rapidly, they'll accommodate. If you make a demand on your muscles to work for longer periods of time, they'll adapt to that demand. The principle of aerobic development works on this principle. Aerobic capacity is an accurate measure of stamina.

Stamina is a natural response to training; therefore, it isn't necessary to spend time developing it before you begin training. In fact, that wouldn't even be desirable, since the best stamina for you is specific to the activity you choose. If you're a tennis player, it's better to play many fast rounds of tennis than to jog ten miles through the park.

Stamina is also a function of relaxation, strength, and suppleness. The natural athlete who has freed himself from the burden of chronic tension will, in his relaxed state, require less effort to build stamina. Suppleness allows greater movement with less energy, because the joints are free of drag from constricted connective tissue. All athletes must develop stamina over periods of time, but the natural athlete is ahead when he begins.

It takes time to get into shape. Lawrence Morehouse, a UCLA researcher, and other colleagues have found that in four weeks of inactivity, you can lose 80 percent of your conditioning—and in four more weeks of progressive training, you can also regain 80 percent of your top fitness after being totally out of shape. If you progress very, very slowly, it may take more than four weeks. If you push it, you might shorten that time, but you're going to hurt.

"Hurt" is what most athletes are accustomed to doing. Athletics is one of the only fields where masochism is made to appear respectable. You have the perspective by now to know that *you don't have to hurt in order to feel good.* The jogger who has trained for two weeks, running one and a half miles on level ground, and then decides to start running hills for three miles is forgetting natural order. Learn to develop stamina *gradually.* You'll inevitably get to whatever level of fitness you want, depending upon how long you continue progressive training—*not* how fast you do so. "Getting in shape" can be a thoroughly invigorating, pleasurable activity. It will require some adjustments and even discomfort as your body adapts to an increased demand, but if it hurts a lot, you're "pushing the river."

Though the best training for stamina is *specific* practice of your sport, you can practice general endurance during pre- or off-season, such as strength training or aerobic activities. That way you can begin regular training without exhaustion, aches and pains, or injury during your first days of enthusiasm. In closing the section on developing physical talent, we come to an essential postscript.

Athletic injuries and how to avoid them

Injuries are the worst thing that can happen to an athlete. The pain involved is the *least* of it. A single injury—whether developed over a period of time or all of a sudden—can undo all the time and energy of training, and perhaps end a career permanently. Injuries inevitably leave a trace of tension and fear in the body. They're a traumatic setback . . . and never seem to happen at a convenient time. Injury is the negation of the primary purpose of sport—health and well-being.

Injury is *always* the result of a fundamental weakness in a mental, emotional, or physical area of talent (or a combination of these). "Accidents" aren't really accidents. If you injure yourself, or if someone else injures you, *someone* wasn't paying attention, was upset, or wasn't physically prepared. (In fact, these three variables account for all "accidents" in daily life which can be linked to human error.)

Thus, mental clarity and attention, emotional stability (and abiding motivation), and physical preparation are the three best insurance policies you'll ever have . . . and they don't cost a cent.

Acute injury, resulting from an impact (a fall, a collision, a blow) or from another force (such as a torque or twist) which is beyond the body's limits of tolerance, is actually much more rare than *chronic* injuries, or those developed over periods of time, through improper training or insufficient preparation. Natural training helps to eliminate both kinds of injury by undermining the causes of them.

I'm going to create a patsy, a "fall-guy," in order to highlight some of the major causes of injury—mental, emotional, and physical:

Jerry sprained his ankle, and couldn't understand how this "accident" happened to him.

Mental factors. Jerry is distracted very easily, either by his own thoughts or by activities going on around him. He has a self-concept of being a "klutzy guy." He has a habit of criticizing himself mercilessly, and has latent tendencies to punish himself through pain. He has serious conflicts about competing, and the season is about to begin.

Emotional factors. Jerry's motivation to play goes up and down. Sometimes he's really "fired up" and sometimes he wishes he were on the sidelines. He's always been afraid of contact sport and any risky maneuvers, so he tenses up at the wrong times. Sometimes he hangs back and hesitates. Sometimes he gets angry and stomps around the gym, paying no attention to what's going on.

Physical factors. Jerry's ankles are stiff and relatively weak. Because of general tension, he's insensitive to fatigue, and pushes himself too far some days; he's overweight, and in poor general condition.

Jerry should be glad he only sprained his ankle.

Looking back on the few injuries I've done to myself in the athletic arena, I see the reasons clearly now and have been able to avoid further trauma since. How many of us "knew but didn't do." We knew we shouldn't push that hard that fast—but we did. We knew we shouldn't lift a heavy object like that—but we did. We knew we shouldn't have played when we were tired—but we did.

The natural athlete acts on his clear intuitions; therefore, injuries are extremely rare in the natural process of training. He fully recognizes the possibility of injury for *him* as a price of insensitivity and inattention. His safe, gradual, and natural training reflects his approach to daily life.

With a wish for a safe journey, we close the section on physical talent.

The three centers and whole-body talent

You've now surveyed the meaning of talent and how it can be developed across the three centers of mind, emotions, and movement. When I first came upon this whole-body approach to athletic training, I was astonished to realize that paying attention to something like breathing could open the way to better balance or greater effective strength, due to the breath's influence on body and mind and emotions. Yet it is true—it works. Natural training cannot be approached by attention to the physical body alone; we must delve into and clarify the subtle realms which are really the foundation of our lives.

Power and balance are, of course, necessary in every sports endeavor. *Absolute* stability can be achieved only through combined focus of mind, emotions, and physical practice. The state of being *centered*, when the mind is quiet, the emotions open, and the body relaxed/energized, gives you, quite literally, a better connection with the earth. This connection is essential, because all the forces you exert must come from the earth. You are only the transmitter—whether you swing a baseball bat, throw a football, or swing a golf club. The following exercise allows you to experience this whole-body connection to the earth:

▷ ―――――――――――――――――――――――――――――――

Tense   **Stand stiffly, breathing in the upper chest, with shoulders raised. Feel the tension. If any current dilemma is bothering you, think about it.**

Have a friend standing in front of you reach under your armpits with his hands and lift you an inch or two off the floor as you hold onto his arms with your hands. Remain stiff and tense with shallow breathing as he lifts you.

(It doesn't matter whether or not your friend is actually able to lift you at any time—as long as you both can feel the difference between the first and the next attempt.)

Centered   **Next, shake loose and relax. Relax your mind by feeling the breath pleasantly in your lower belly. Feel physically heavy and stable, like a lazy cat or a sleeping baby. Let your shoulders hang down. Imagine your entire lower body is hollow, and then filled with water.**

Resting your arms on your friend's arms, ask him to lift you in the same way as before—slowly, without any sudden movements. If you maintain this relaxed, centered focus, it will be very difficult, perhaps impossible, for him to lift you. You feel rooted to the ground.

――――――――――――――――――――――――――――――――

This "rooting to the ground" is what the ancient masters of t'ai chi perfected, through attention to whole-body talent. No one could push them over; they could apparently harness "supernormal" forces and effortlessly toss opponents into the air. For them, it was only natural. . . .

Practicing physical development can take you far, but only to a point—and that point is short of enriching your daily life. As we close this section, "Developing Talent," I urge you, as your training progresses, always to keep in mind what the natural athlete knows: that physical ability alone, without development of mental clarity and emotional energy, is a hollow accomplishment.

Part Three

On The Road

Moving with spirit

Your map is complete. You now have the insight and perspective to know what you want to do and how to do it. You will begin to experience an internal guide, showing you the way to your individual aspirations safely, efficiently, and surely. Willing to trust the natural laws, you can be patient and wise.

Nature's way is ordinary— absolutely ordinary and easeful. There is no necessity for heroic struggles. To take things gradually and to flow with them expresses the natural course. This book is only a different approach to the ordinary. I've simply presented ordinary elements of common sense to you—like the fact that strength, suppleness, sensitivity, and stamina have something to do with physical talent. In the same manner, I intend to continue showing aspects of the ordinary that might be left unexamined (and therefore unused).

If you had taken six months or a year to read this far into the book, and if you had aligned your training with the principles and practices outlined, you would already have completed the most difficult part of your training. You'd have perfected the massive foundation for that iceberg floating unseen beneath the waterline; you would now, in fact, represent the raw material of the natural athlete.

Now you are potential energy, potential action. In the coming sections, it's time to test all the philosophy and advice where it counts—in action; it's time to apply the principles through plain old perseverance and guts. Yet, it's not just how hard you work that counts, but how *smart* you work. You know that it's natural for you to progress as time passes—but your *strategy of training* can determine whether that progress is slow and tedious, or fast, effective, safe, stable, full of ease and pleasure. You finally have a chance to apply your energy in motion, up the mountain path. Let's hit the road!

7 TECHNIQUES OF TRAINING

Smart, fast, and fun

All training technique is only a shadow of the natural laws. Without natural alignment, you'd only find the various techniques confusing. However, as you begin to embody these laws through conscious practice, you'll become a master of technique without ever reading another *how to* book. The natural athlete, already grounded in the basics, can really appreciate a time-saving tip.

Every teacher has an armory of advice and tips relevant to his specific sport. Many of these tips are useful and can be applied to more than one activity; therefore, it's wise to find a good teacher or experienced friend who has gathered these specific gems of guidance.

What I want to convey in "Techniques of Training," however, are the fundamental, general techniques of learning any and every form of movement. No matter what activity you practice, you'll be able to apply the following approaches and strategies.

Warm-up

Our lives are filled with cycles and with periods of transition. Your growth from infancy through childhood, adolescence, and adulthood required many transitions into increasingly advanced modes of behavior, responsibility, and understanding. Birth and death are the Great Transitions. Graduating from school, beginning a livelihood, getting married, raising children, and retiring are all lesser but typical examples of changes in our lives. Life is a series of changes—sometimes smooth and orderly, sometimes unexpected or chaotic—from minute to minute, day to day, year to year.

Your life will be enhanced as you develop the capacity to recognize these periods of transition, major and minor, and make conscious use of them. I used to act "snarly" with my wife when I arrived home from work, until I realized that all I needed was about fifteen minutes alone to slow down, take some deep breaths, read a few chapters in a favorite book—before I was ready to listen happily to her news of the day. That fifteen-minute transitional period from the hustle-bustle rhythm of work, to the mellow atmosphere at home, was necessary.

Most people's transitions are scattered and unconscious. As in that chaotic, emotionally turbulent transition called adolescence, we seem to be the victims rather than the masters of change. Most of us haven't even handled getting up in the morning or going to bed at night with any conscious enjoyment. Our transitions seem to consist of throwing cold water on our face and stumbling into the next activity come what may. Our minds, emotions, and physical rhythms may still be adjusted to an earlier frequency as we begin a new activity requiring much slower or faster vibrations. No wonder we sometimes have difficulty coping with new situations.

Transitions are in-between periods. When you leave work and are driving home, you're in-between. When a golfer has hit the ball and is walking down the fairway, he's in-between. Learning to enjoy and make use of these in-between periods will even out our lives. Most of us tend to fall asleep or blank out during in-betweens, so that life consists of jerky motions, stops and starts—like changing from first gear to fourth, and fourth down to first, without an even flow.

You *can* make your transitions fully conscious and far more effective and pleasurable by noticing when you're moving from one kind of activity to another, which may require a different mental, emotional, or physical approach.

Instead of leaping out of bed in the morning, you may find it useful to set the alarm fifteen minutes earlier, giving yourself time to glide into the kitchen, put some water on for herb tea, read for a few minutes, look out the window and take some deep breaths, say hello to a new day. You may wish to include some light calisthenic or stretching movements or a walk around the block before breakfast as part of your morning transition. This is only a random suggestion; the main point is to create conscious transition rituals for the hours, days, months, and years of our lives.

Nowhere is the transition ritual so crucial as in the world of athletics. *Warm-up* is a transition gesture on the way to the Intense Realm of conscious exercise. What could be more natural? Each day's game or training session is an island unto itself. What you did yesterday and what you hope to do tomorrow don't exist; today is what counts.

Your daily warm-up serves as a buffer zone between the day's prior events and the moment of truth in the athletic arena. A proper warm-up serves to prepare you for the unique demands of sport, and helps you avoid those days when nothing seems to go right. Warm-up is equally important for body, mind, and emotions; therefore, it is more than a few jumping jacks.

The mental warm-up consists of determining a clear course of action for the day. You'll want to choose realistic goals, based upon the circumstances and your energy level that day. Further, it consists of turning your attention to the place of practice, leaving all the day's cares and concerns at the door. Finally, you want to cultivate the proper attitude of respect and gratitude—the right mental "set"—for your activity. (This is the original basis behind the Japanese tradition of bowing upon entering and leaving the practice hall.)

A gymnast requires a transition between two pieces of apparatus, because of the different qualities of each. You wouldn't, for example, carry the same mental set from uneven bars to the balance beam—nor would a ballroom dancer approach a waltz and a disco dance in the same way. Runners and swimmers cultivate a different approach to sprinting and distance events; golfers need different mental warm-ups for driving and putting. Mental warm-up, then, gives you the clarity and proper approach to make good use of the day's activities.

Emotional warm-up might begin with a few deep, calming breaths. You may wish to recall the initial excitement you first felt about your sport. Choose your emotional goal—focus on what fires you up about training. Imagine yourself succeeding at your goals; picture yourself winning because of a good practice day. Feel how much you can gain from some wisely directed energy.

Note: Mental and emotional warm-up might seem to be long and involved, but actually they can take place almost simultaneously, at the speed of thought. The whole process might take place in the space of five slow, deep breaths or a moment of quiet contemplation as you make your transition. Many athletes do something like this subconsciously. The natural athlete does in consciously and strategically, in order to control and amplify his direction and energy for the day.

Physical warm-up should be a definite period, set aside. It doesn't have to (and in fact, probably shouldn't) be a long, involved process. Yet it is a time to get the body literally *warm*, oxygenated, fully awake, free of cobwebs (including both mental distractions and physical sluggishness), and loosely relaxed. Don't rush into warm-up. There is never any need to shock the body. Remember, it's *warm-up*, not the main event.

You may start out feeling absolutely clogged up and asleep. Don't let that discourage you. Some of my all-time best workouts began awfully. It just took the body longer to warm up on those days. Your body is in some ways like an automobile. You wouldn't want to start a cold engine, then race off at top speed. The oil (or blood, in your case) isn't warm and flowing yet.

Start easy with some light cardiovascular movements such as light running or skipping rope or calisthenic movements which incorporate deep, full breaths. Suck it in and blow it out. Move every joint. When you're feeling warm, you may wish to do some stretching. Include ankles, knees, and wrists.

Warm up and stretch at a relaxed pace, even if you're late. Make time for warm-up so you never have to rush. Blow your warm-up, and you may have blown your game. And remember that a few light stretching and deep breathing exercises as a warm-*down* are also very useful.

Learning how to learn

Perhaps when you were a child, you had the opportunity to play in an empty lot, just after a fresh snowfall when the bare earth was hidden by a smooth cover of snow. Maybe that winter you were the first kid on your block to blaze that first straight, clean pathway through the knee-deep, crunchy carpet of white.

As it happens, the neurological pathways you blaze when you learn a new movement pattern are just like the paths through that snowy field. The white carpet is your nervous system; the pathway is a neural one, and it represents a specific movement pattern or skill.

After all your preparation is done, learning a skill consists of blazing the correct neural pathway and motor response, then stabilizing that pathway for consistency. This applies to any movement pattern, simple or complex, whether running, jumping, swinging a bat, throwing a ball, or turning a triple somersault.

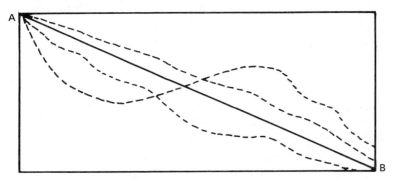

I use the image of the snow-covered lot (above) because it graphically represents what happens in your neuromuscular system when you are learning a new skill. The solid line from A to B shows the perfect execution of a skill. If line A–B is your first attempt at the skill, it means that you were totally prepared—mentally, emotionally, and physically—and were thus ready to do it correctly the very first time.

Because most of us are not perfectly prepared, our first attempts are generally represented by the curving dotted lines above. Then we gradually home in on line A–B. This homing-in process takes varying amounts of time, depending upon the approach to learning.

Your first attempt at a new skill is the most important one, because you've formed no previous pathway. You're likely to follow the first path you make, the next time . . . and the next time. Every time you take the same neural pathway, you'll stabilize and reinforce that motor response *whether it is correct or not.*

Every time you let yourself practice a movement incorrectly, you're increasing your ability to do it wrong. It follows that you want to repeat the correct movement pattern as much as possible and to avoid repeating an incorrect pattern at all costs. Therefore, a fundamental rule of learning is this: *Never repeat the same error twice.*

We know that errors are a part of learning. You will make errors. However, in order to avoid stabilizing the errors, you have to make consciously *different* errors each time, toward the correct pattern. If you make different errors, you don't become accustomed to one; you don't habituate yourself to any single incorrect movement pattern. This is a very important point, because one of the prime causes of slow learning is repetition of (and thus habituation to) one incorrect motor response. You get used to swinging the bat too low; you get accustomed to arching in a handstand; you begin to feel comfortable shifting your weight to the wrong foot on your golf swing.

As you consciously make each attempt *different,* you're simply exploring the many possibilities for error as you home in slowly to the straight path, the correct way, without forming bad habits.

Awareness and practice

If you practice hitting a thousand golf balls every day but *really pay attention* to only two hundred swings, then you're wasting eight hundred swings a day—and in fact, those eight hundred semiconscious swings may be doing you more harm than good, because, as just discussed, you can form bad pathways without noticing it—like walking through the empty lot in your sleep.

Practice doesn't make perfect; only perfect *practice makes perfect.* Proper learning technique consists not only of attempting the correct pattern, but avoiding the incorrect one. While practicing, remain fully aware in your mind and in your body of *every* attempt. If you make an error, never just "do it again." Take a moment to be fully aware of *what went wrong;* if you don't know, you'll just repeat the error. Then make a strong attempt to do something different.

The stages of practice

Most of us assume that if we want to become skilled, we must practice the skill over and over, many times. This is not necessarily true. Most beginners tend to practice *too much* at first. If you're a beginner at a particular skill, you'll probably have a low level of feeling awareness at first. You don't exactly know what it should feel like or what you're doing. Therefore, don't practice too many repetitions, or you're likely to develop incorrect patterns. Instead, begin with a *few* repetitions, maintaining *intense concentration* and *real interest.* You may continue while concentration and interest are strong; but if you begin to repeat an error, or if real interest and attention start to fade—if your approach becomes casual—then stop, and come back to it later on. Practice is like gambling: You have to know when to quit. When you find that you can consistently repeat the correct pattern, only then should you begin to do many repetitions for endurance and stabilization.

Following this principle, I taught myself to juggle three balls in a very short time. I'd try each progression, beginning with one ball, then two, and finally three, only four or five times each day. Working for five minutes a day, in five days I taught myself to juggle three balls. It's very true that some people might learn to juggle three balls in one day, by practicing for an hour or two. What I want to emphasize, however, is that the way I suggest, aligned with *natural order* and realistic psychological dynamics, will allow you to learn *correctly*. Many "fast learners" also pick up little compensations and poor habit patterns. They may learn it fast, but they don't necessarily learn it *right*. Take the time to learn it right, and you'll save time. There's a big difference between learning and learning correctly.

As you practice, stop for a moment between each two attempts. "Check yourself," take a deep breath, shake loose, and relax. Feel awareness tingling through your body, out to your fingertips and toes. Feel your connection to the earth. Then continue.

Learning, then, is not just a matter of casually (or fiercely) doing a move over and over. That may build stamina and muscles, but it will not necessarily develop the straightest path to natural ability. What you require is a *strategy of training*—employing insight and concentration in place of mechanical repetition. The following techniques and principles make up that strategy of effective learning.

Overcompensation is the single most valuable aid to rapid learning you're ever likely to come across. Here's why: When you're performing an incorrect movement pattern over a period of time, you're going to become comfortable with that pattern. Any changes—even toward the correct pattern—are going to feel "strange" because you're not used to them. *When you're wrong, what's right feels wrong.* Because of this principle, *corrections tend to be insufficient.* Your attempts tend to cluster around your old habit.

For example, if you're learning to hit a baseball and have formed a habit of swinging too high, you'll tend to continue swinging high. Even if someone tells you to swing lower, you'll only correct a little bit—or it will feel "all wrong." Maybe you'll swing a little lower than before, but it will *still* be too high.

Therefore, recognizing the law of balance, you have to apply overcompensation to your practice, and work *both sides* of the movement. You have to make a determined attempt to swing "much too low." When you attempt this, it's best if you actually swing under the ball. After working both sides, you'll know where the middle is. (Most likely, though, in trying to swing "too low," you'll connect with the ball.)

The principle of overcompensation—or working both sides—applies to elements of timing, balance, accuracy, and force, in every possible sport or movement art. It works on the same natural gyroscopic principle that allows a guided missile to home in on target quickly, by moving from one side to the other, until it finds the middle. "Finding the middle" is what effective learning is all about.

▷ **FASTER LEARNING THROUGH OVERCOMPENSATION**

Take a lemon or other unbreakable fruit. Toss it behind your back and up over your shoulder, catching it in the same hand, in front of you.

I'm going to assume this is a new skill for you. You can throw the object over the same or opposite shoulder of the hand in which you hold the object. The main object here is to make conscious use of *overcompensation*. Work on one variable at a time. If you threw too far left, then on your next attempt, throw too far right. If you then throw too far behind you, make sure you throw way in front of you. Then you'll find the middle.

Using this principle, you should be able to learn this tricky skill in just a few minutes. You can then apply the same technique to your music, arts, dance, or sports endeavors. But like many other athletes, you may experience resistance to working both sides. You may feel that it's a "waste of time" to try to do something wrong deliberately. You may feel impatient just to do it right the next time, and want to avoid another wrong attempt, even on "the other side." If that's the case, I hope the reasons behind the strategy of overcompensation are now clear, making its time-saving usefulness obvious.

If you are not capable of working both sides, due to insufficient strength, suppleness, or other qualities which would enable you to overcompensate, then it's back to basics. You need more preparation, or you'll only ingrain the error more deeply.

If you feel acutely uncomfortable or even fearful of working both sides because it "feels too strange" (especially if you're engaged in a high-risk sport), that's normal. If you're a high diver and you keep underthrowing a dive, you may be a bit hesitant (or completely petrified!) at the prospect of overthrowing the same dive. It may be the same hesitation for a gymnast, etc. But in such cases, I can only say that the principle still applies—and you can make use of it or not. You will have to overcome fear in addition to any other resistance you may feel—but I think you'll find that it's worth it.

To sum it all up, if you wish to learn successfully and rapidly, *you must be more interested in learning a movement than you are afraid of crashing.*

Ideomotor action and mental practice

Your powers of imagination can enhance old skills and help you to learn new ones. This is possible because of the interaction of mind and muscle. In the negative sense, turbulent thought can impose muscular tension, as you've seen. On the positive side, clear mental imagery can—even without actual movement—develop correct muscular responses. This can be demonstrated with a simple experiment:

Tie a small weighted object (like a ring) to a six-inch length of thread or string. Let the object hang by the string, held by your thumb and first finger. Hold the string still, then begin to imagine that the ring is swinging back and forth, back and forth. Continue to imagine this, and watch what happens.

Next, while the ring swings back and forth, imagine that it is going in a circle instead; see the results.

This little test demonstrates the phenomenon of *ideomotor action*—that for an image of movement, there is a subtle, corresponding muscular impulse. If you relax the body and imagine yourself performing a movement correctly, the muscles respond. Ideomotor action is a key principle behind mental practice.

I remember one study of mental practice, using a group of sixty beginning basketball players. The group was split into three groups of twenty each.

• The first group physically practiced shooting baskets from the free-throw line, by attempting a specified number of shots in a specified time, for a period of two weeks.

• The second group was asked to practice *mentally* in exactly the same fashion—imagining themselves shooting baskets.

• The third group did unrelated activities during that same time period.

Everyone in each group was tested at the beginning of practice, and after the two-week period. As expected, the third group didn't improve. However, those who *mentally* practiced improved almost as much as those who trained physically.

The moral of that study is not, of course, that we should begin practicing from the living-room couch—but that mental practice can be very useful as a supplement to physical practice. I gained a reputation as a "natural" when I competed on Cal's gymnastics team, because I would seem to learn difficult movements "effortlessly" on the first try. What my teammates didn't know was that I would dream about those moves the night before, and perform them in my head all day, before actually attempting them. When I finally did the movement, it felt as if I'd done it already, many times before. This helped me to overcome fear, too.

Especially in some situations, mental practice has distinct advantages:

▪ It's absolutely *safe*—unless you mentally practice your golf swing while driving down the freeway.

You can do it *anywhere*. However, be careful with this. I once imagined myself doing a trampoline routine, while sitting in a dull political-science lecture. As I practiced, my arms made "waving gestures" as I "twisted" and "somersaulted." The professor stopped his lecture, and all eight hundred people in the hall strained for a look at the "guy in the front row, having a fit."

▪ There's no fear of failure in mental practice, because it can be free of error; you can perform brilliantly. There are exceptions to this rule, too. One of my gymnasts at Cal would consistently fall off the balance beam. As surely as the sun rose, as regularly as Monday followed Sunday, she'd fall off. She fell on weekdays or weekends, rain or shine, in practice or competition, without discrimination.

One day, out of sheer desperation—for her safety and my peace of mind—I suggested that she try mental practice for a while. "Go through five or ten routines perfectly, in your head," I said, feeling that perhaps in this way she'd develop a good habit.

I busied myself with the other gymnasts, until later,

when I glanced over and saw her sitting there, brows knitted with concentration, eyes shut tight, whispering to herself, "Damn! Oops . . . oh, damn!"

Puzzled, I asked her what was the matter. She replied, "Oh, nothing, coach. It's just that I keep falling off."

• Another advantage of mental practice is that it's free. If you take those private lessons twice a week instead of three times, or an hour each day instead of two, you can spend the rest of your time practicing in your imagination. You really get your money's worth.

• Mental practice means that you are automatically concentrating. You can do casual physical practice by just letting your body go through the motions without real attention. Not so with mental practice. Because of this, it is difficult. You have to develop your capacity for visualization and imagery—but once you do, your efforts will reap rewards of learning.

Mental practice can be used if you're ill or injured, or at odd moments during the day when there's nothing much to do. It beats thinking about your problems—and you can get a jump on your favorite opponents.

As you imagine yourself doing well in competition or practice, this will also serve to dissolve negative self-concepts. There exists evidence to suggest that athletes who improve faster than equally prepared counterparts simply put in more mental practice time. When someone would ask me how I learned a particular stunt, I'd joke, "Oh, I think about it a lot."

Mental practice also explains the common phenomenon of athletes returning to a sport after a layoff, only to find that their technique has improved—or the athlete who is having some trouble with a skill on Friday and after a weekend layoff finds the skill improved on Monday, with no "practice" in between. In just thinking about the movements, it's possible for you to improve because you don't practice any errors. Mental practice is more *efficient* than physical practice; it's also more difficult (mentally).

The main requirement is to stay entirely relaxed, so no other muscle tensions interfere with the proper response. You can lie down, or sit quietly. Of course you have to have some kind of "feel" for the movement before practicing it in your imagination. Once you know how it should feel, practice it repeatedly in your mind. Like anything else, mental practice takes practice!

SLOW-MOTION PRACTICE

Test 1. Hold your right hand in front of your face, so you are looking into your palm. Quickly move your right arm out to the side, turning your palm outward, and stop. Notice how you were aware of only the beginning and the ending of that movement.

Test 2. Now repeat the same sequence, but this time, move your arm and hand in slow slow-motion—as slowly as you possibly can. Let it take a full minute. Be aware of the relaxation of the arm and hand muscles. Notice how each finger turns; clearly see the different angles of your hand, as if for the first time.

In this test, you were clearly aware of the movement of your arm and hand in its entirety, from beginning to end.

Slow-motion practice gives you the time to be aware of *every part* of a movement, whether it's a baseball or golf swing, a javelin toss, or a karate punch. You can sense the complex parts such as weight shift, coordination of body parts, etc. Since most unconscious errors occur in the middle of a movement sequence, slowing the movement down can have surprising benefits in ease and speed of learning. Mistakes that were hidden can become painfully obvious.

I even discovered, after a period of slow-motion practice,

that I could move faster than ever, because in moving slowly, I became aware of tension and was able to let it go. Without tension, it's possible to move with blinding speed. (Tight guys, I have noted, move like dinosaurs.)

Slow-motion practice is like studying slow-motion instant-replay films of training, except that you're also *feeling*—not just seeing. You can apply this technique to virtually every sport or movement form. It applies particularly well to activities like golf, baseball, tennis, handball, and so on. In gymnastics, I'll often carry the athlete slowly through a somersaulting movement so she can become aware of every part of turning over. Slowing down practice expands your awareness, and eliminates the blurred blind spot encountered in rapid movements. You can be very creative in applying slow motion to different activities. (If you figure out how to apply it to skydiving, I'd like to hear about it.)

Slow motion *works*, and it's fun. Like the practitioners of t'ai chi, you may even discover that slow-motion sport is a form of moving meditation.

And now a word about the *beginning* and *ending*. In highlighting the midpoint of the movement sequence, I didn't intend to slight the start and finish because, in fact, both beginning and end are keys to a correct *whole*. Sometimes it isn't practical to work slow motion—for example, in learning a cartwheel. In cases like this, it's useful to pay strict attention to a perfect beginning and ending position. You may not have any idea where you are in the middle, but if the beginning and ending positions are just right, *the middle will take care of itself*. That's why so many coaches instinctively emphasize the correct follow-through.

Don't just swing the golf club, hit the ball, and move on. Hold the ending for a moment and check your position, your balance, the position of your arms, head, and body.

When I teach golf, the first emphasis is balance and whole-body centering; then I show the best beginning and ending positions. These things form the basis of a consistent swing.

The physical application of beginning-ending awareness is that if you complete a movement and find that you're in the wrong ending position—for example, if in attempting a somersault, you find yourself on your nose instead of your feet—you should move as rapidly as possible to the correct ending position. The next time, you'll find that you won't be quite as far off—perhaps on your ear this time—and you should again move instantly to the correct ending. Before long, you'll simply end in the proper position, and the middle will begin to flow smoothly as well.

Part-whole practice

Any skill, like your car's carburetor, is made up of component parts. If you want to clean a carburetor and find out why it isn't working well, you take it apart and find the trouble spot. It works the same for a movement skill. The entire carburetor—or skill—may be fundamentally all right . . . except for one little part (which can cause imbalance in the whole) but you don't know where it is. That's when analysis comes in very handy.

A good teacher or insightful student can dive to the source of the problem, undistracted by symptoms. Once isolated, the problem is practically solved.

I've found it useful to teach a new movement skill by breaking it down into its parts—first the beginning, then the middle, then the end. Afterward it's easy to put the whole thing together.

Analysis can also be applied to specific drills which can save time and make learning an entire movement pattern much easier. Instead of isolating your practice to a single activity or skill, it's valuable to practice related drills. For example, divers will often train on the trampoline to learn somersaults and twisting without getting wet. Hotdog skiers will do the same, because they can practice more repetitions with less energy. Pole vaulters can use certain gymnastics drills to learn more efficient ways of working the pole, without being limited to practice on the pole. A baseball batter can practice his swing by standing with his side next to a wall and swinging the bat, feeling his weight shift into the wall just as the bat makes contact. These fundamental drills, which can be created and applied to any activity, save time.

The programming principle

Today, more and more *programmed learning* books are being written. It's possible to learn complex subjects—such as the fundamentals of law, medical terminology, English grammar, languages—through programmed texts. They're based on the natural principle that we will learn easier and better if

▪ We learn in *small steps*, taking it in simple and progressive increments.

▪ We take an *active part*—filling in the blanks.

▪ We get immediate reinforcement and feedback—the answer is shown as soon as we fill in the blank.

▪ We feel successful, because of the small, simple progressions.

Good programmed learning texts are designed around common-sense principles. They make learning easy and therefore fun. I have approached learning—and teaching—using the same principles, and have found them to be of great use to myself and to my students. Any movement can be learned by first taking it apart (analysis), then practicing it in very simple progressions or steps. Programmed progressions allow for a constant feeling of success in which the *process of learning*—rather than a single end result—becomes the goal.

In the future, some patient and meticulous teachers will design programmed texts for movement activities. Until then, however, you can be creative and make up your own programmed progressions.

Imitation: the ultimate technique

After all else is said and done, we end by returning to the way children learn—by copying. Kids are masters of imitation. And copying is the most instinctive, simple, and natural way to learn. We could all imitate beautifully once, like the talented infant . . . before we learned that it was "bad" to be a "copycat," that we were supposed to do our "own work." (I was fortunate enough to have parents who never discouraged my interest in imitation. They told me that it was fine to copy people, as long as I was certain their qualities were worth copying. I extend that advice to you.)

As a matter of fact, we can learn far more than athletic skills through imitation. As a young man, I tried out many ways of talking, gesturing, relating with people, and even styles of living—by imitating special qualities I admired in the people I met.

I've never met a single person who didn't have at least *one* quality I admired. Caligula, for example, had some very fine qualities, along with some crippling ones. So did every villain, lout, or hero in history.

Everything and everybody has a mixture of qualities—virtues as well as defects. Look for the good in everyone you meet, and that person becomes your teacher. Imagine how smart you can become, with everyone you ever meet becoming your teacher, without knowing it. The garbage man can teach you before breakfast, while the hairdresser or newspaper boy can inspire you after lunch.

In order to be teachable—to learn—you must be able to admire and be grateful for the qualities another possesses. Push your envy or insecurity aside. There will always be people with strong qualities. Envy will only isolate you; appreciation can help you incorporate those qualities into your own life. Open your eyes with awe. Be like a humble child.

Learn by observation, appreciation, and imitation. Soon the best qualities will fit you like a glove, and you'll always have something fine to wear.

If you want to learn a skill, find someone who is very skillful. Watch this person carefully. Study his (or her) musculature and movements, facial expressions, arms and legs. As you watch, feel *yourself* moving in the same way; then practice your ability to imitate.

Your ability will improve with practice. If you wish to copy a drawing of an accomplished artist, you may not be able to reproduce it precisely at first, but with practice, your copy will improve. You can practice copying anytime during the day. Begin by learning to imitate other people's movements—their styles of walking, talking, and gesturing. (A side benefit of this practice is that you learn to observe better and pay more attention to others.) Remember that even the most creative painters began by copying—over and over and over.

Of course you must first be *prepared* in order to copy well. If some guy can lift two hundred and fifty pounds, you can't imitate him unless you've developed your strength; if a ballerina lifts her leg high into the air, you must have the necessary suppleness and muscular control before you do a perfect imitation. Even babies, the master copyists, are limited in what they can imitate. This underscores, once again, the vital importance of preparation before you attempt to make full use of the techniques of learning.

Imitation, then, is *the* fundamental way to learn movement patterns, once the preparations are complete. Even if you aren't able to copy someone perfectly, your attempts will increase your awareness of what qualities you still need to develop—in order to reproduce that which you so admire. In the meantime, copy what you can.

I'm convinced that imitation is the master technique of learning. It bypasses intellectualization; it's learning-in-action. I was able to become a world-class athlete by first recognizing the most admirable movement (and mental and emotional) qualities in the athletes around me, and then, with unswerving commitment, imitating those qualities . . . until they were mine. *You can do the same* if you're really interested.

If you feel that you've not yet attained a high level of expertise, it may be that you've not made the best use of your powers of imitation. If this is true, it's probably due to one of the following reasons:

• You may *not be sufficiently prepared* to copy well. (If so, back to basics; develop your talent.)

• You may experience *unconscious resistance* to copying someone else, because of a belief that you must "live your own life" or because you don't feel that you could ever imitate an expert's skill level (still acting on a low self-concept) or because you don't like acknowledging that someone else may have a quality which *you* don't presently possess. If the latter is the case, you've just got to swallow your pride. . . .

• You may be copying the wrong people, or the wrong qualities. This is an ever-present fear of parents, who feel that their children may "pick up" the wrong qualities if their kids don't have proper playmates. Exposure does have a lot to do with the qualities you develop as a child and as an adult—since you can't imitate that which you've never seen. On the other hand, exposure isn't enough. You have to develop your higher instincts, to listen to your ideals in order to recognize the finer qualities in others. It's not always easy; if it were, we could all become models of the world's great artists, saints, and sages.

(The more insight you have into your own strengths and weaknesses, the more you'll be able to look clearly and deeply into others. Then you'll no longer be so susceptible to "picking up" weak qualities through unconscious imitation—and you'll begin to see qualities in everyone worthy of imitation. In this way, every person you ever meet can become your teacher.)

You are better at copying than you may imagine:

Have a friend face you, and hold his arm in an unusual position. Copy his arm position, as if looking in a mirror. Have him take another position, perhaps with both arms askew. Imitate that. Then mirror his whole body posture. Try the same thing as he moves very slowly.

You'll find that you can mirror your friend with a high degree of precision, with a little practice. Why not apply your ability to imitate throughout your sports activities and daily life?

The techniques, principles, and strategies that I've outlined so far are practical ways of learning how to learn. They are all designed to guide you on your own journey.

I've only offered words and concepts and images on paper; you have the capacity to bring it all to life. Using awareness as a lever, you can apply the keys that open the right doors for you. Begin with the techniques that you remember—the ones that make the most sense to you. If you use even a single technique to its fullest extent, it will enhance your game—and can enrich your life.

Now we turn to competition—to the game itself—in the Moment of Truth.

---

8 COMPETITION

Success in the moment of truth

In the living room, restaurant, or locker room, when the subject of competition comes up, there seem to be three primary attitudes: One group of people admires the competitive ethic as a Great American Tradition—"what made this country strong"—along with capitalism and the credo of the individual spirit, making it on his own, taking credit for his own successes and failures.

Another group, philosophically inclined to "peaceful coexistence, harmony, and cooperation," avoids competition as dehumanizing. This group prefers exclusively cooperative endeavors, without an "us" and a "them"—gravitating instead to New Games, other cultures, looking to the Orient for inspiration.

The third group doesn't give much of a damn either way.

Competition does have its positive and negative faces. On the positive side, it's the athlete's ultimate test of reality, demanding his full involvement, energy, and spirit. Competition can be a valuable and exciting source of self-testing rarely found (to the same extent) in other facets of society. (Sometimes I think the hustle-bustle business world was just invented by competitive athletes, past their physical prime.)

Competition brings out the athlete's best and worst. The strengths which emerge can be reinforced and the weaknesses corrected. Competition is one of our last formalized opportunities to face a genuine Moment of Truth—the final frontier of romance and adventure. Drawing the best from a man or woman, competition can be a model for positive, assertive, and realistic efforts in daily life. Athletes tend to be successful, because they know the value of organization and hard work; they know that life doesn't just hand you everything. Therefore, sports can be a source of valuable life lessons for young people.

Competition can even be a form of movement meditation in which all your attention and feeling is focused on the present moment, free of random daydreaming. And it's an enjoyable form of entertainment for millions of people, as well as a source of inspiration to many boys and girls. Many of our most intelligent athletes are admirable role models.

On the other side of the coin, we must consider the negative effects of competition on many people. There are few "winners" and many "losers." Competition reinforces these polarized words—"winner" and "loser"—as if the world were divided into two camps, dependent solely on athletic prowess, with no gradations in between. Children who play highly competitive games emerge as losers more often than winners, in spite of all our well-intentioned slogans about ". . . it's how you play the game."

Competition tends to breed strife and opposition. (Often before collegiate football games, pictures of the opposing team are posted outside the training-room doors, so the men on the home team can get to know and "hate" their counterparts, in order to "run over" them in the game. Such a practice does tend to encourage, to say the very least, a less-than-ideal attitude in daily life.) In some competitions, I've even seen competitors laugh or cheer when a member of the opposing team falls.

Competition may reinforce a simplistic, black-and-white way of thinking and looking at the world, with "winning" as the only respected goal. It encourages some unfortunate values: "keeping up with the Joneses," comparing ourselves to others to determine our own worth. Day-to-day improvement would seem a more accurate measure of individual or team achievement than who beats whom, yet we see that the recognition, awards, and trophies don't go to the "most improved" athletes or teams. If your team plays poorly, while the opposing team is playing even worse, there would seem to be little cause for self-congratulation by the "victors." That's why a badly played game leaves you feeling let down, whether you are participant or observer, and regardless of who wins. If your team plays its best ever, but a superb team outscores you, I can't find any cause for disappointment.

Competition doesn't always have to be a bad thing, and in any case, athletes don't have any exclusive on the competitive state of mind. In many nonsports activities, such as modern dance, ballet, or painting, you will find individuals who are jealously competitive with each other. I've known professional athletes, on the other hand, who viewed their game as a cooperative "mutual-teaching session" between two teams. Steve Hug, one of the all-time best American gymnasts, never really competed *against* anyone, because he didn't have that kind of mentality. He simply did his best, measured by his own rather than anybody else's standards of excellence. Because of his approach, he was one of the most centered athletes and successful competitors I've known.

Even in "man-on-man" sports, such as basketball or football, it is possible, and often advantageous, to view one's opponent as a teacher, who serves you best by doing his utmost to outdo you. In the same way, you can best serve this comrade-in-sport by outdoing him. Once you view competition in this way, you will always try to win, but without a trace of the hostility and negativity which too often characterize the competitive mentality.

Winning and losing can be completely arbitrary. I once won a world trampoline championship, and have carried around that title ever since. What really happened, however, was that I had a good day, and at least two other athletes, who might have won on another day, just weren't hitting as well. To say that I was "better" than they in any absolute terms would bear no meaning. I was only "better" for that one competition. Luck, biorhythms, and for all we know, astrological signs may all have a lot to do with winning and losing. It seems wise not to take the whole thing too seriously.

Free of the combative state of mind, you find no opponents—only people like yourself, striving toward excellence. Unfortunately, it appears that some of the more "successful" coaches are frustrated war heroes, treating competition as fervently as if they were going to war against real enemies. Such intense rivalry probably does motivate teams, but at what price to the mind and emotions?

The Moment of Truth itself—the competitive enterprise—*is* an exciting stimulus to excellence. Yet its purpose ends when the final gun goes off, and time is out.

Once you catch a fish, you no longer need the pole; when a butterfly is trapped, you no longer need the net; when meaning is grasped, you no longer need the words—

and when competition is over, you no longer need the scores. But what a big deal we make after the game is over! Colleges and professional teams preserve past scores like prize butterflies, pressed into books. So many people become preoccupied with numbers, statistics, titles, victors. During the game we must let the game command our attention so that we can feel its energy and excitement but after it's over, what purpose have numbers? What does it all mean?

The natural athlete has a way of forgetting the game's outcome the moment it is over—but he remembers its lessons. The usual athlete learns no real lessons, because he's still stuck in the outcome.

A natural athlete can't afford to revel—or despair—over the past. The ancient Olympic wreaths, made of laurel, reminded their wearers that fame is fleeting, and glory fades. The only lasting value in the competitive experience are the lessons we learn and keep alive.

Ultimately, it makes no difference whether you or I praise or belittle competition. It's here, and has great acceptance and following. It's a reality. If you do compete, you might as well give it your best shot, as you would any other aspect of life.

In the heat of competition, theories of learning how to learn—and the principles of nature—may seem only vaguely relevant or interesting, and the gymnasium may seem the place for action, not philosophy. But philosophy is going to develop the athletes of the future.

Athletes, coaches, and teachers can only study biomechanical techniques for so long. They can only work so hard; they can only eat so well. Eventually, it's going to be the more subtle elements of talent—those invisible qualities of mind and motivation—that are going to determine the new champions. Work will always be a key element, but it will be psychophysical work, imbued with the qualities of the natural athlete, that will make the difference. And if insight into the lessons of nature and qualities of talent can help to develop a world champion, it can also help your game—no matter what your present level or experience.

In the competitive arena, there will always be those more and less skilled than yourself. Some may be near the top of their own mountain; others are perhaps struggling up the first steep paths far below. As you continue onward, make use of competition to stimulate your efforts along the way, but be careful not to become too preoccupied with the peak, high in the distance—or with those athletes who are far ahead; if you do, the pleasure of the climb may be lost in craving for the goal. Keep your own natural pace. Whether your path on any given day is clear or rocky, the real and only measure of your achievement can be found in answer to a single question: "Have I done my best today?" All winning, losing, titles, and fame fall into the shadow of that question.

Physical preparation for competition: overload and cutback

In the Moment of Truth, you are moved to focus all of your present capacities of mind, emotion, and body on the game. Like the natural athlete, you can play as if your life depended upon your fullest effort—yet laugh at the outcome. Armed simultaneously with humor and intensity, you'll be able to harness your fullest energies. And *fullest* energies are what is necessary. Often in the heat of competition you'll press your body beyond its normal capacity. The psychophysical response to competition, including release of adrenaline into the bloodstream, hypermotivation, and sharp focus, enable you to outdo your everyday capacities. Therefore, you must be prepared for this temporary jump in capacity—or your body will tell a sad and painful story the next day. . . .

The primary tool used by experienced coaches and athletes is *overload and cutback*. As the name implies, the method is to overload the demand before competition, then cut back just before the day arrives.

The significance of this method is far more than physical; it also results in a psychological feeling of confidence, ease, and security. If you are about to run a five-mile race and you ran eight miles through the hills last week, you're not only going to be physically prepared, but you're going to be feeling very relaxed and self-confident.

Though no coaches I've met have a name for this method, its use is almost universal. For example, in gymnastics, the athlete will overload on the number of repetitive routines, going as high as eighteen routines in a workout. After that, the few routines he (or she) performs in a competition will seem like a snap—even if the athlete feels a little sluggish.

The rule of thumb is usually emphasis on quantity as the season reaches a peak and, just before the championships, emphasis on less quantity, more quality. The exact timing varies from sport to sport. The important thing is to build up to more than you'll be called upon to do in competition.

The following overload techniques can all be useful:

• Training with a weight vest, ankle or wrist weights (or just heavy shoes).

• Running greater distances than necessary, faster than necessary, or up hills.

• Practicing without the use of one sense—eyes closed, for example—so the other senses become more refined.

• Working deliberately under *poor conditions*. For example, jugglers may practice in dim light or windy conditions; ice skaters may train for a while on poor ice, in case they meet these conditions in competition;* martial artists may practice their skills in the ocean surf or in a pool underwater.

• Increasing a normal demand. For example, a baseball batter can have the pitcher throw fast balls from three-quarters the usual distance. If the batter can learn to hit those pitches, it will be far easier to connect with full-distance throws.

How much overload you practice depends upon your own temperament, capacity, and activity. The main point is to practice *some kind* of overload, then cut back for competition.

Emotional preparation

It's entirely normal to feel skittish, nervous, or anxious before a competition. Those around you also feel the same way, though some have learned to act confident and calm. Whether you experience the jitters as shaky knees, upset stomach, compulsive yawning, low energy, hyperactivity, or emotionalism, you'll want to know how to deal with this unnerving phenomenon.

Understanding the nature of the precompetitive body helps to overcome—and to use—the symptoms of nervousness. Remember that the competition is a ceremony—a special occasion when you are, in reality, tested. You *should* feel nervous! Your body is responding to an appropriate psychophysical preparation for a unique demand.

Because of your mental focus, adrenaline is released into the bloodstream. This glandular secretion stimulates a release of simple sugars into the muscles for extraordinary

---

* It is always valuable to duplicate any poor conditions under which you may have to compete. This is a major factor in competitive success; you must be able to adapt to all conditions.

activity; your heart begins to beat faster; your breathing mechanisms are stimulated (thus the yawning). The muscles are trembling with readiness and energy. Don't fight it. If you're just sitting there, waiting to go, you will feel shaky knees and stomach butterflies, because the body is ready to run, fight, jump, go . . . right *now*. Therefore, if you feel these symptoms before you actually need them, you can control and use the flow of adrenaline by moving. Do some jumping jacks, run in place, or do a few push-ups. All the body's responses are designed to enable you to move faster, stronger, and better.

If your mind is filled with negative motivation ("I'd better do well or it will be embarrassing . . . my parents [girlfriend, boyfriend, teammates] are depending on me—I can't screw up! . . . I hope I don't break my neck . . ."), then you will experience the jitters as fear, weakness, or even paralysis.

If you work on positive motivation ("Now is my chance to come through in a real pinch . . . my parents [girlfriend, boyfriend, teammates] are going to be proud of me. . . . Wow, look at that crowd . . ."), then you'll experience these nerves as excitement and anticipation.

If you're predisposed to tense muscles, then the body's response to psyching up can be more tension; if you've learned to relax, then you can channel and direct the extra energy.

Like the natural athlete, you can become a natural competitor too. With a realistic approach, you'll see clearly that you *tend to perform in competition as you did in practice*—sometimes you'll be a little shaky, but usually you'll do a little better. With a realistic approach, you'll be free of illusory expectations of sudden miraculous improvement—and equally free of unrealistic fears of bombing out. You'll understand that results are in direct proportion to preparation. This perspective gives you more respect for training, so you make the best use of your time, and never depend upon adrenaline alone to pull you through.

More seasoned athletes usually fare better in high-pressure competitions. They're able to control the adrenaline response; they don't walk around gawking at the other athletes, but focus on their own efforts; they're familiar with the competitive procedures, and have developed rhythms of warm-up and energy expenditure.

Experience, however, isn't always measured in time. Experience comes from having learned the lessons of competition and of training. Some athletes gain a great deal of experience in a relatively short time. Other athletes may compete for years and never be seasoned, because they aren't open to the right lessons.

One sure sign of the experienced athlete is that he *treats training and competition with the same respect and intensity.* When he trains, it's with the same mental focus and determination as if he were in competition; when he competes, he's as relaxed and easygoing as if he were practicing.

Psyching up and psyching out: the mental game

Competition tests all your capacities; physical skill is only one part of the game. It's not unusual for the most conditioned athletes to come in second or third, because they haven't mastered the mental game. A physical expert can be weakened and distracted if he's susceptible to emotional flightiness or mental fuzziness. The ancient samurai warrior recognized that a razor-sharp mind and emotional calm must precede physical skill . . . if he was to live a long life.

Competition is a psychophysical duel, in which you have the opportunity to test your serenity and one-pointedness as well as your reflexes. It follows that within the rules of the game, it's perfectly appropriate to psych-out your friendly opponent. It's all part of the psychophysical nature of sport. Teach your opponent something about the inner game. The psychological strategy can add a whole new dimension to competition, and can turn a contest of brute strength and speed into a chess game.

The psychological game requires mental acuity, refined judgment, and plain old intuition. If you casually mention to your opponent that you notice his socks are frayed, it can drive him to distraction; phrase it another way, and you may fill him with determination to wipe you all over the court.

My father told me a story about a tennis-player friend of his named Jack, who was a master at psyching out his opponents. Jack was going to have an important match with another guy who was compulsively punctual. Well, Jack offered to pick him up at his home and drive him to the match "so they could have a friendly talk before the match." The fellow agreed, and the trap was set.

Jack "couldn't seem to find his way to the courts" that day. Oblivious of his opponent's frantic signaling, advice, and map waving, Jack confidently told him that he knew the way, as soon as he could "find the Safeway market." Well, they pulled into the parking lot about one minute late. The officials were ready to go. Jack was calm and apologetic—his opponent was completely frazzled. He could hardly connect with the tennis ball . . . and gave Jack the match on a platter. At least he may have learned a good lesson about compulsive punctuality. He certainly learned never to ride with Jack again.

I learned about the psychological strategy the hard way. I'd flown to Southern Illinois University to compete in the final trials for the U.S. Trampoline Team—three finalists who would fly to England for a major competition. My primary competition for this trial was Frank Schmitz, an exceptional athlete. Frankie offered me the hospitality of his fraternity, which I gratefully accepted.

He was the absolute gentleman. He befriended me like a brother and insisted he'd find "any old place to sleep," giving me his bed and electric blanket. He showed me all around his campus and was generally the nicest person in the world. He was totally sincere—and I had lost the match before it had begun.

Anyone who's uncomfortable with psychological strategies may not yet fully recognize the psychophysical nature of sport—and is missing half the fun of competition. If you play, you might as well learn to play in the psychophysical realm.

Never get so involved in psychological strategy, however, that you lose your own center and forget your primary objective—to present your *own* best effort. It's not helpful to put someone mentally off-balance if, in the process, you fall off-balance too. The best strategy is your own unshakable confidence and calm, free from anyone else's influence. Seeing someone who is apparently a tower of strength can be incredibly distracting to the competition.

Above all, even as you play with your full determination and power, remember that the game will never be more than a game. The lessons it offers are absolutely important, but the game itself is only play. (Every game makes *somebody* happy.) Armed as you are now, with your background and perspective, you've *got* to be a winner . . . even if you should sometimes lose.

9 THE EVOLUTION OF SPORT

New games for new athletes

Since ancient times, when leaping over bulls, fighting lions, and hitting rocks with a stick were the latest fashion, sports have come a long way. Never entirely static, sports evolve with the passing of time, reflecting the dominant, mainstream values of the culture in their rules, structure, creativity . . . and degree of violence.

Some sports, such as ice hockey, approach the deadly traditions of the gladiators, who often fought to the death for the entertainment of packed Roman stadiums. Other movement forms, such as gymnastics, sport acrobatics, diving, and ice skating, are evolving into performance arts, with all the elegance and aesthetics of the ballet.

It's wonderful that such a variety of sport forms exist to meet the interests and needs of different people. Yet, sport deserves very close scrutiny, because it does far more than passively reflect values—it also helps to shape and reinforce ways of acting and being that may have positive or negative carry-over in daily life.

Sports and games are fun. They're invigorating and boisterous; they encourage teamwork, timing, cooperation, and organization; athletes are stronger and healthier in many ways than nonathletes. Everyone recognizes the benefits of running, jumping, swinging, swimming, throwing, catching, somersaulting, and balancing. At the same time, however, sports can predispose you to chronic pains in the shoulder, elbow, wrist, lower back, or ankle joints. Athletics can, when pursued intensely, develop specialized or imbalanced bodies—effective on the playing field, but disabled in daily life.

Any influence so central to our lives, both physically and psychologically, must be approached with an attitude that is far more than casual. We know that the benefits of sport probably outweigh the possible liabilities. But instead of resting with that statement, we can look to see if there's a way to enhance the benefits of athletics further and to diminish the liabilities.

A natural, healthy approach to sport can be expressed by two questions:

1. Does this sport effectively contribute to the physical and psychological well-being of the athlete?

2. Does this sport develop heightened capacity for daily life?

In light of these two questions, we can, in the same way we would look at our own strengths and weaknesses, assess the relative value of our own sport—and see if we can't make some welcome changes.

The broken records of each new Olympic Games reflect new heights of achievement. Yet, from the psychophysical perspective, training is still at a rudimentary level. If we look at the realities of high-pressure competitive sport today, we can see many examples of a "moving violation" of the natural laws of body balance.

Many athletes sustain themselves on food a goat wouldn't touch; we still specialize in pursuits which develop huge, beefy muscles; many of our favorite pastimes create imbalances in the natural symmetry of the body (including such games as tennis, bowling, golf, and baseball). It's not that such activities must be abandoned, but they should be balanced and complemented by proper training.

Even with all the new techniques of scientific measurement and systematic methods of physical development, our approach to athletic training is still imbalanced. We've only begun to touch the surface of the potential benefits of athletics. Today's age of more sophisticated awareness may mark the beginning of a new tradition, in which sports are consciously designed for overall psychophysical development—to supplement or even replace the worn-out or outdated games of the past.

The most obvious way of changing sports is through modifications of the rules.

Changing the Rules. The rules of today's sports have developed over long periods of time. They're reflections of our philosophies of what is fair and just and right; they indicate the current state of our wavering tolerance for violence, and our striving for beauty and spirit. Any changes in rules must therefore be undertaken with the greatest care.

If we desired more violent confrontations, we could equip our ice-hockey players with brass knuckles. If we desired less combative hostility and more interteam cooperation in football, we could require that the opposing linemen, ends, and running backs have to spin three times around one another before beginning their normal pursuits.

At this point I want to suggest one basic rule change which would render some of our most popular games more interesting, more challenging, and far healthier for our bodies:

Symmetrical training

Golf, tennis, bowling, baseball, and many other sports which make primary use of one side of the body are marvelous games. However, they are, without doubt, debilitating to the symmetry of the body, so vital in natural alignment to earth's gravitational pull. By a simple rule change, we can increase the value of these games and eliminate their major liability: We require these athletes to make equal use of both arms.

There are several arguments against such a rule change: First, equipment modifications would be necessary in many cases. Second, the stars of today would have to make some fast adjustments in order to remain stars. Third, those of us who were just beginning to feel proficient would have to undergo a temporary "klutzy" period again.

Now let's look at the benefits of *symmetrical training*:

• Chronic pains of elbow, back, or shoulder would be lessened or eliminated by working both sides, since each side is given a periodic rest.

• You could practice more without fatigue.

• You would be more versatile in many situations, thereby spicing up your game.

• You would eliminate the sport's postural imbalances, resulting in freedom from one-sided tension in the arm, shoulder, and along the spinal cord, and better alignment in gravity.

• If you were getting a little stale, this new challenge is guaranteed to bring you to life.

• Some research shows that learning a skill on one side increases learning facility on the other, and can, in fact, help eliminate old weak habits.

The rule of symmetry, if applied to our one-sided sports and games, would have benefits to health and well-being. This new rule would be fundamentally aligned with the natural laws. It seems clearly beneficial, but the change hasn't happened because of resistance by the participants. That resistance is something we all have to cut through in order to join the force of evolution and change. That brings us to the second and most important way you can personally influence the evolution of sport—by changing your approach.

Rethinking sports

Casey Cook, an inspirational diver I coached at Oberlin College, told me that the sport of diving evolved for him as he began to view his movements in terms of energy awareness. He felt as if he were "sculpting" energy as he somersaulted his way into the air, forming lines of energy he could almost see. As he learned to shape the direction of energy flow, he felt he was playing a new game, on "nature's team," with the board, the air, and the water as teammates. He was no longer a lonely body, bouncing on a board, mechanically spinning, attempting to knife through the water for a judge's reward. During leisure hours if he played baseball or threw a Frisbee, he still enjoyed this sense of energy flow and graceful harmony with the natural forces. Without a single rule change, Casey had "changed" the sport of diving.

Two professional football players—Chip Oliver and

David Meggysey—both quit the professional ranks at the height of their careers, because they realized that the sport as they had played it was not good for the body or spirit. After studying yoga and other integrative disciplines, Chip suddenly realized that football simply ". . . hurt too much." Later, each of these men was drawn back into the sport they loved, but with a new approach to the game—using football as a means to blend with others, to practice symmetry, to master relaxation-in-movement, and to use the sport as a lesson in living.

If sport were only practiced in a vacuum, isolated from the rest of life, then we might accept the chronic psychophysical problems as a price the athlete must pay—but sports activities cannot be separated from daily life. In order to benefit daily life, the world of sport must be a way of life; it must develop all the best within us, in harmony with our highest ideals.

Eventually, along with refined physical training, athletics will consist of natural dietary disciplines, the training of mental one-pointedness, and the use of emotional energies. The natural laws will become the new slogans on the locker-room wall.

Perhaps there is no single ideal athletic form. That seems appropriate, because no one sport is ever going to appeal to everyone. Yet certain key elements will be of great benefit to you if they're incorporated into your total athletic training. If one or more of these attributes aren't included in your sport, work them in on the side in order to balance your development:

Mental

• Encourages attitude of blending and harmonizing rather than collision or linear opposition.

- Enhances ability to "see" flow of energy.
- Develops sensitivity to the body's needs instead of callousing over pain signals.
- Demands full attention and concentration.
- Contains sufficient pressure or risk to arouse thoughts of fear, anger, etc.—so they may be transcended, thereby developing traits of daring, calm, etc.

Emotional

- Encourages friendly, cooperative interaction rather than isolation or self-preoccupation.
- Serves as a laboratory to understand yourself and others, in an atmosphere of mutual help and support, teaching-learning with one another, and giving up, on occasion, individual rewards, preferences, or glory for the good of the group.

Physical

- Balances development of the body; neither too much nor too little muscle or fat.
- Demands (and develops) suppleness of all body joints.
- Develops cardiovascular fitness and whole-body stamina.
- Aids muscular symmetry and postural alignment in gravity, placing stress factors on both sides.
- Enhances body's connection to the earth through dynamic calm, relaxation-in-movement.

Many of the above attributes may not automatically be part of your game, but you can make them so by your approach. If you notice an important area lacking—and there are weak elements in every sport—you can still take a natural approach to training by finding suitable activities to balance your game. A football player might take up t'ai chi; an ice-hockey ace might practice hatha yoga; a baseball player might practice ballet—and a yogi might take up karate.

Many of us search for the ideal game. There is none. All you need to do is enjoy what you're already doing. Moving from one sport to another, feeling alienated, is a lot like moving from one country to another, or from one spouse to another. You're only going to find a different set of benefits and liabilities. There is probably no need to move from where you are if your present sport or situation feels right for you. Take a short vacation, and return with fresh appreciation; make the best approach you can, and supplement your basic approach so that you meet all your physical and psychological needs.

Games of the masters

If the peak cannot be reached without losing touch with the body, or if it is reached . . . [through alienation] of the body, then new games must be invented.
—Dr. Michael Conant, U.C. Berkeley

The natural athlete is no longer anxious, no longer struggling, and no longer eager for victory at all costs. Because he feels no alienation from any game, he gravitates to new and experimental forms of exploration and fun. We end this section with a preview of sports to come, a vision of tomorrow. The four new sports which follow by no means exhaust the possibilities; I only offer them as samples:

 I. SLOW-MOTION RUNNING: BALANCING TODAY'S PACE

Object: To finish the race *last*.

Rules:

1. Competitors begin on the starting line, facing the finish (a wall) 10 yards away.

2. At the signal "Go!" all runners must begin to move continuously—without stopping forward motion—in a direct line toward the finish.

3. Each step must be a length of at least 12 inches (measured by 9 parallel lines, drawn between the starting line and finish).

Discussion. Slow-motion running is a far more challenging sport than may appear at a glance. In trying to reach the wall last, the best athlete will have to move with awesome slowness. This requires excellent balance, sensitivity, the ability to relax—and a kind of dynamic patience. This ability reflects an entirely new kind of psychophysical stamina—a quality of body-mind balance rarely explored in usual sports. Slow-motion running is a form of moving meditation, similar to that practiced by practitioners of Zen meditation. If you try it sometime, you'll appreciate its challenging nature and meditative repose. It's a perfect balance for the speedy pace of most of today's athletics.

II. ENDURO-GOLF: THE VALUE OF SYNTHESIS

Object: As in regular golf, to finish the game with the fewest strokes—but also in the shortest time.

Rules:

1. All the regular rules of golf apply, including the etiquette of replacing divots, etc.

2. The competitor is timed with a stopwatch, from the first drive to the final putt.

3. For every minute elapsed from the start to the finish, one-half of a stroke is added to the golfer's score. Thus, the faster he finishes, the lower the score.

4. There are 3 different events under which an enduro-golfer may compete: (a) 3 holes (for sprinters); (b) 9 holes (for intermediate-distance duffers); (c) 18 holes (for marathon golfers).

5. Each golfer may carry as few or as many clubs as he wishes, but is allowed no carrying aid.

> (However, if someone wishes to combine golf with the best traditions of another sport, such as motorcycle or race-car driving, you can see the possibilities—souped-up golf carts.)

Discussion. Golf may be one of the finest games ever devised in the Western world. It's the closest thing we have to a Zen art. Golf demands the natural qualities of nonresistance and balance, and allows an athlete to blend with a beautiful variety of natural scenery; golf is a vacation within the city. Where many other sports seem to demand strength and brute force, golf demands relaxation, controlled and graceful momentum, and "letting it be." The variety of challenges found—the type of shots required—encourage awareness of energies, sensitivity to the environment, and the ability to remain centered and one-pointed.

However, many people cannot see the point of spending five hours of a beautiful day "hitting a little white ball around a field." Golf doesn't seem to offer sufficient exercise. . . .

Enduro-golf combines the best elements of golf with the cardiovascular training of track. The synthesis of the two will make a fascinating event to try—or to watch. Imagine sprinting like crazy down the fairway, carrying your three most prized clubs, and in an instant (no time for dawdling) stopping, estimating the distance, making yourself totally calm and centered, swinging as if you had all the time in the world . . . then tearing off down the fairway again. (Oh, and don't forget to replace your divot.)

III. GYMNAIDO: THE EVOLUTION OF A SPORT

Object: As in other gymnastics events—to score as close as possible to a perfect 10 on every event, through sufficient endurance and skill, flawless technique, and aesthetic style and presentation.

Rules:
1. Men's and women's events have been combined, so that men and women can compete with one another on an equal basis. (This is possible with the

new events, because in gymnastics, athletes handle only their own body weight.)

2. There are four events:

Floor-beam exercise.   A *combination* of floor exercise and beam. A padded beam, 5 inches wide, adjustable between 2½ and 3½ feet high, is placed along the inside border of the padded, resilient floor-exercise area.

Each athlete performs a 2-minute routine of his own devising to musical accompaniment (which may be any music at all, except vocal). In addition to the regular tumbling, dance, and floor-exercise work, the gymnast must travel the complete length of the beam 3 times, with turns, balance, and aerial elements, including a flowing mount and dismount for each passage.

Trampoline.   A 12-millimeter bouncing surface allows any performer to achieve sufficient height. The trampoline is completely padded all around with a 6-foot border of 8-inch-thick pads, and springs are covered.

15 bounces total, judged on the basis of difficulty (4 superiors and 7 mediums required), height, form, and control.

Double horizontal bar.   The gymnast performs a horizontal-bar routine, but is required to pass through the air from one bar to the other at least 3 times during the routine. There is safety padding beneath the bars.

Sport acrobatics.   Each team shows 6 routines of aesthetic pair work. 3 routines consist of pairs of the same sex (may be male-male, or female-female), and 3 routines are mixed pairs. Each routine is done in harmony with suitable music (anything but vocal). Each routine must show balance, tumbling, dance, strength, all in tempo and in harmony with one's partner.

Discussion. Gymnastics offers a combination of mental and physical demands found in few other sports. *Gymnaido,* which means "way of harmony through gymnastics," offers the best combination of events in gymnastics and sport acrobatics to give the body balanced, healthful development. All four events are universal spectator favorites, and will draw large audiences to support the athletes. The four events consolidate all the primary benefits of gymnastics (strength, suppleness, stamina, and sensitivity—particularly refined kinesthetic sense). Men and women would be afforded the uncommon social opportunity to train together, as equals. With less apparatus to buy, more programs could be set up around the country.

IV. T'AI CHI-DO: REFINING THE SUBTLE

Not competitive in nature, this activity needs no rules. Its only structure is based upon the practitioner's understanding of natural law. T'ai chi-do incorporates the central elements of two of the most refined martial arts: t'ai chi ch'uan and aikido.

T'ao chi, which originated in China, places greater emphasis on subtle, slow-motion softness and sensitivity (though on advanced levels, one can move with blinding speed, and demonstrate its potentially deadly qualities).

Aikido is entirely nonviolent in intent—never designed to injure another deliberately—and emphasizes positive energy flow through relaxed movement to deflect, channel, and control an attacker's energy, through the use of graceful throws and wrist locks. Aikido contains a lighthearted blending of movement and energy and practice in falling and smooth rolling (not included in t'ai chi).

When we think of self-defense, we usually imagine defense from a human attacker. This imagery is limited. Through the practice of t'ai chi or aikido, one learns the art of defending himself from, by blending with, everyday problems and stresses—from tension, fatigue, and lowered resistance. These are the real enemies, not human beings, and these are enemies who attack us with far more frequency. Aikido rolls are especially useful to people who may have occasion to fall and want to do it smoothly and creatively.

T'ai chi-do combines aikido movements of evasion and blending with the slow-motion meditative awareness of t'ai chi. These movements can be practiced alone as a dance, or with partners, at varying speeds, from lightning-and-thunder to the slowness of shifting sand dunes. T'ai chi-do offers a blend of two worlds.

The uses and designs of sport are limitless. Recognizing that athletics is a mirror of daily life, you can bend your creative energies toward improving and evolving the benefits of conscious movement.

Athletics can be a means of enjoyment, recreation, psycho-fitness, biofeedback or, as we will increasingly discover, a way of transcendence, of unity—a path to a spiritual life. The door is open. You have only to walk through.

Part Four

At Journey's End

Achieving unity

The Chinese sages, in talking about the River of Life, the delicate, ephemeral existence of the butterfly, or the way of trees in the wind, were paiting pictures, drawing metaphors, all pointing to the natural laws . . . the source of all human wisdom. All the Teachers of mankind have pointed to the same thing—that in order to grow truly, we must reintegrate the wisdom of our life experience with the open-eyed innocence of childhood.

In order to achieve or realize his natural unity with his universe, man must first attain unity within himself—by balancing and harmonizing body, mind, and emotions. Throughout history, in different cultures, Masters of Life have appeared who understood more than a man learns by life experience. They had realized this unity and, in their wisdom, created Great Teachings. These Teachings—including many of the great religious and esoteric practices from Sufism to Cabala, Taoism, and Zen to the yoga systems of India—are counted among the major spiritual traditions of mankind. Taken all together, they represent whole-body teachings of mind, feeling, and action.

Our technology is a kind of functional knowledge and certainly has its uses. But we have much to learn, and to integrate from the comprehensive world-view of our global heritage of wisdom. The West has the opportunity to evolve very rapidly, beyond mere technology (which predominately represents the mind, subordinating both feeling and body vitality). As a Chinese sage might put it, "The blossoms of our wisdom are just beginning to open in the sunlight of time."

Our time is coming. This is the potential Age of the Natural, Total Athlete. Passing through the age of material wealth, in our disillusion with empty technological achievement, it becomes possible for us to transcend symbolic solutions, and finally dedicate our journey to the

Great Goal, which cannot be fully articulated, because it is beyond intellectual symbols; it is feeling and attention, the perfect balance of body to mind. In that balance is the discovery beyond words, beyond illusions or images of happiness, beyond the security we normally seek or know.

The way to the goal is the path upon which you now walk. Athletics is the yoga of the West, emerging today. All that is required is a different perspective—using training as a *means* rather than an end.

Your map is complete. You can see that the laws of nature, the laws of athletics, and the laws of living are the same. There is no escaping from these laws; they are your only freedom. Finally, you see that to become a natural athlete, you have to become a natural human being. And that means living a life of positive energy, discipline without extremes. It means loving in principle and in action, when you would rather not love. It means being happy whether you have a good reason or not. It's awesomely difficult, because the way of the natural athlete means abandoning all your old habits, your self-preoccupation. But if you see the possibilities of such a way—if you see the necessity for a new approach to athletics, then you can do it. You *will* do it, in time. Then, what perhaps began as a search for a little skill improvement becomes a much bigger game after all. Athletics takes off its cap, shakes out its hair, removes its numbered jersey, and you see only a blinding light; it becomes a yoga of spiritual unification. That is what the top of the mountain truly represents.

Your training can literally change the quality of your daily life. As the three centers develop, open, and balance, you begin moving, feeling, and understanding differently . . . and life becomes free.

10 PSYCHO-FITNESS

Rebirth of the master athlete

The athletes we admire on television are the end product of refined physical education. In the course of their training, they've reached a high level of physical fitness. They have randomly achieved a certain capacity for concentration and perhaps emotional stability. Still, many of the experts may be effective in the gym or on the turf, demonstrating fantastic skills, but unaware, unstable, or undisciplined in the mental and emotional affairs of daily life. We've all seen such *experts* at the Olympics, at Wimbleton, or at Pebble Beach. You can see many experts, but you'll see few masters.

The *master* is a product of psychophysical training, a whole-body athlete who demonstrates unity in all his actions. He (or she) has a well-rounded capacity for life—in any environment, in any endeavor. The expert may shine in the competitive arena, but the master's light shines everywhere.

One day in feudal Japan, a master of the tea ceremony was on an errand in the marketplace, and collided with a foul-tempered samurai. Immediately, the swordsman demanded an apology for the "insult" in the form of a duel to the death.

The tea master was in no position to decline, though he had no expertise with swords. He asked if he could complete his obligations for the day before meeting the samurai for the duel. It was agreed that they'd meet in a nearby orchard, later in the afternoon.

His errands completed early, the tea master stopped to visit the house of Miyamoto Musashi, a famous swordmaster and painter. He told Master Miyamoto his situation, and asked if the swordmaster could teach him how to behave so as to die honorably.

"That is an unusual request," replied Miyamoto, "but I'll help if I can." Detecting an air of composure about the small man standing before him, Miyamoto asked him what art he practiced.

"I serve tea," he replied.

"Excellent! Then serve me tea," said Miyamoto.

Without hesitation, the tea master took his utensils from a pouch and began, with the utmost serenity and concentration, to perform the graceful, meditative ceremony of preparing, serving, and appreciating o-cha, the green tea.

Miyamoto was very impressed by this man's obvious composure on the afternoon of his death. The tea master was apparently free of all thoughts about his waiting fate, a few hours hence. Ignoring any thoughts of fear, he focused his attention to the present moment of beauty.

"You already know how to die well," said Miyamoto, "but you can do this. . . ." Then Miyamoto instructed him in details of how to die honorably, ending with "it will probably end in a mutual slaying."

The tea master bowed and thanked the swordmaster. Carefully, he wrapped his implements and left for the duel.

He saw the swordsman waiting impatiently, anxious to get this petty killing over. The tea master approached the samurai, laid his implements down as gently as he would a tiny infant—as if he expected to pick them up again in a few moments. Then, as Miyamoto had suggested, he bowed graciously to the samurai, as calmly as if he were about to serve him tea. Next, he raised his sword with but a single thought in his mind—to strike the samurai, no matter what.

As he stood, sword raised, mind focused, he saw the sword expert's eyes grow wide with wonder, then perplexity, then respect, then fear. No longer did the swordsman see a meek little man before him—now he saw a fearless warrior, an invincible opponent who had mastered the fear of death. Raised over the tea master's head, glinting blood-red in the sun's last rays, the samurai saw his own death.

The sword expert hesitated for a moment, then lowered his sword, and his head. He begged to apologize to this little tea master, who later became his teacher in the art of living without fear.

And leaving the bushes from where he had concealed himself, Miyamoto stretched with pleasure, yawning like a cat. Grinning, he scratched his neck, turned, and walked home to a hot bath, a bowl of rice, and sleep without dreams.

The story of the tea master and the swordsman illustrates how a master of one art can master any art, because he's mastered himself. The master represents psychophysical maturity, which quietly shows itself in every aspect of life. Physical skill is only one aspect of his game, and a relatively unimportant part, at that. He knows that the ability to do a full-twisting somersault, to drive a golf ball, blast a tennis serve, pitch a no-hitter, or slam-dunk a basket is not going to change the quality of his life fundamentally.

Physical improvement is fun, it's satisfying, but it is not the primary goal for the natural athlete. Physical skill comes naturally, but incidentally, to the master. The master's skill is only a byproduct of internal development.

Professor Eugen Herrigel related stories of his own experience in learning Zen archery while on sabbatical leave in Japan. A typical Westerner, he was at first puzzled by the enigmatic words of his teacher, who spoke of "spiritual shots," "shooting with no mind," and "letting the arrow shoot itself." The master would sometimes say, "Yes!" sometimes when the shots missed the entire target, yet once he criticized Herrigel severely after he'd hit the bull's-eye.

As time passed, Herrigel began to understand the internal emphasis of the Zen art. The master told him that the real bull's-eye was internal, and that the object of archery was to use the physical practice to train the mind.

The object was not merely to release the arrow, but to release all thought—even the thought of "I." Shooter, shot, bow, arrow, and target all had to fuse into Emptiness. That was the spiritual shot—even if it happened to go wide of the physical target.

The master told him on another occasion that "egoic archery," no matter how skillful, was the wrong target— that the mere expert would remain incomplete in his understanding.

As it happens, one Zen archer recorded twelve hundred bull's-eyes in a row. Herrigel's own teacher, he reported, was able to shoot one arrow into the target's center, then split that arrow with a second, like Robin Hood—only the teacher did it in pitch darkness.

The movement master in daily life

The movement master may remain unnoticed by those around him. Because he does everything naturally, he doesn't clash, and has no desire to stand out. If you observed him closely, you would see an ordinary man. Over a period of time, though, you might begin to observe that he always seems relaxed, calm, alert, and open to circumstances, without effort. He brings a kind of peaceful humor to life. He has no need to play a righteous or holy role, or to act "together." He *is* together, and so he can appear a clown; at his whimsy. He has seen it all from the inside and has nothing left to defend.

The movement master—male or female—may practice a craft, musical instrument, athletic or other art form. In any case, every movement he makes receives his undivided attention. Thus, he has a presence and certainty about him which radiates security; others follow, although he has no particular desire to lead. When he washes dishes, he is *only* washing dishes; his mind is a washcloth. When he walks, his mind is walking; when he cooks, his mind is a pan of hot food; when he sweeps, his mind is a broom.

The master creates a ceremony out of every moment. He folds clothes, eats, washes his face, or sits down with the same attention *we* would give to a championship game. His decisions have a three-dimensional quality, balanced among rationality, intuition, and gut instinct. Therefore, his decisions always end up "right," naturally appropriate. He's ordinary, yet full of energy, force, and quality. He has the warrior's spirit, bathed in humor.

It was late afternoon when Miyamoto Musashi sat down in a small inn, to eat a bowl of rice with his ancient chopsticks. Chewing slowly, breathing deep in his belly, he apparently ignored three flies buzzing loudly over his head . . . just as he ignored the three vagabond samurai who sat nearby, riveted with greed for the beautiful sword in this "country peasant's" scabbard.

They began to make jesting remarks about his sexual preferences, his mother's background, and his ancestors,

---

hoping to goad him into a fight, kill him, and take the sword. Soon, their insults grew more imaginative and coarse.

Still, Miyamoto continued eating as if he were alone. Suddenly, the three men rose and circled his table menacingly. As they drew near, Miyamoto effortlessly reached into the air with his chopsticks and snatched the three flies, by the wings. Smiling as if to himself, he put the chopsticks down with a grunt of satisfaction, and turned to face his would-be assailants.

They were no longer there. By that time, they had already reached the old river bridge and were running down the road as fast as their legs would carry them.

Miyamoto could have cut the swordsmen in half or turned his table into toothpicks—but here was a warrior with a sense of humor!

Today, such a man would be called a natural athlete, a master of daily life. Men like Miyamoto Musashi serve as reminders that all ways are subordinate to the practice of life.

The expert athlete uses the natural laws to learn athletics; the master athlete uses athletics to learn and align himself with the natural laws.

The lessons of sport

We tend to play at sports in the same way we play at life. Because of the many parallels between the way we approach sport and the way we approach daily life, our training offers many lessons about life, as I have learned both from my students and from experience.

After retiring from gymnastics competition, I began running to stay in shape, starting with a mile and a half. The first day I was sick with exhaustion; the second day I thought I was going to die; the third day seemed worse.

My times improved, but the pain of running continued. I never enjoyed myself—not even a little. One day, a friend ran with me. She told me, "Why don't you slow down a little and enjoy yourself?" You know, it had never *occurred* to me to slow down to a comfortable pace. My temperament had been set on "suffer." If I was hurting, I assumed I was doing myself some good.

I started to pay more attention to other distance runners. They would talk while they ran and seemed to go at a leisurely pace.

I don't know when I first noticed it, but soon I became aware of the same tendency to push myself to the point of discomfort, sprinting through every facet of daily life. I'd eat fast, talk fast, push to read all my studies ahead of time. I had hazy memories of friends telling me to "take it easier," but I didn't quite understand what they meant. My overzealous style had seemed normal to me.

The physical training made the lesson obvious. I learned to apply the natural laws to my life, taking *balance, natural order, nonresistance,* and *accommodation* into account. I could see *action-reaction* taking hold in my reactive dislike to my own self-imposed style of running. Gradually, I learned to pace myself in eating, walking, studying, and other facets of life. For the first time, I started to enjoy life.

I feel grateful to movement training and to my movement teachers—all sources of valuable lessons. My aikido teachers, Robert Nadeau, Frank Duran, and Tom Everett, would always remind their students to relax and to blend with the little problems of daily life in the same way we'd lovingly blend with an attacker. Aikido was useful, because it was a vehicle which allowed me to *practice* the lessons of living, rather than just hear advice.

I hear and I forget.

I see and I remember.

I do and I understand.

Hidden within every experience is a lesson. The Way of Athletics makes these lessons more visible. In learning to move, you are also moving to learn.

Create your own inner athlete

It's difficult for anyone to see his own imbalances clearly—in order to correct them—unless he has a standard, a frame of reference with which to compare himself. We all tend to use our own values and style as the norm; we ourselves are the yardstick by which we measure what is appropriate. Therefore, we all see our own actions and values as justifiable, reasonable, and right. The natural athlete—if he's to get anywhere beyond his own beliefs—needs a more comprehensive perspective.

As you learn to observe yourself realistically in your attempts to function fully, freely, and happily (in sport and in daily life), it may become clear that you don't necessarily represent the perfect balance of qualities. You may find that you don't even come close. With this understanding comes the first real possibility for growth, transformation, and change, because you then become interested in trying different ways, even if they're uncomfortable at first.

One way to help yourself along on the path of growth is to create—from your own natural intuition—the *Ideal Athlete*. This Ideal becomes your inner teacher—a constant inspiration and guide. The benefits of such a mental exercise will be in direct proportion to the energy and attention you invest. Sit down where you'll not be disturbed for at least half an hour or more. Internally, you're going to paint, sculpt, and shape your Ideal Athlete from the material of your mind.

Begin by picturing what this Master Athlete looks like, including height, build, features. Do you want a male, a female? What sport, if any, does this Master specialize in? Give him/her a name.

Imagine how this Athlete stands and moves. Look at his degree of relaxation. Pay particular attention as you create his mental traits and emotional calm. Give this Master Athlete a personality, as if you were creating him for a novel. Create your ideal balance, using any models you may know in life or imagination.

Give to this Athlete all the insight, courage, humor, and realism you'd consider ideal. Imbue him/her with every kind of physical, mental, and emotional quality you feel the Natural Athlete possesses.

Once your creation is complete, you have a teacher who will never be absent. You have an inner example, a source of inspiration. Take this Athlete with you whenever you train. This Master can even be useful to you in daily life.

For the time being, your inner athlete will serve as a frame of reference during practice. You can check how your ideal would move-feel-behave in each situation, and note your feelings, thoughts, and actions in comparison. In this way, your errors and imbalances, previously hidden from your gaze, will show themselves.

You can become this Natural Athlete you've created. You cannot grow or shrink, but you can do a great deal to shape yourself into this ideal. It's a matter of developing each quality in yourself that seems weak or out of balance, in comparison to the qualities of the Natural Athlete within you.

If you're out on the tennis court and something happens that incites you to anger, you may begin to dramatize . . . but then . . . you see that your inner athlete is calm and unperturbed. You immediately see what you're up to. Gradually, eventually, you'll become more aligned to your ideal—until you become that ideal.

This system isn't magic; it requires attention and awareness. But it *does work*—if you do. Begin your creation now; it's well worth the effort.

The art of living . . . with good form

One chilly October night, high in the Sierra Nevadas, I sat with a friend and talked as we stared into the crackling fire. Shadows danced across the trunks of the giant trees around us. Beyond, the world seemed in shadow. Only our quiet voices broke the muffled silence. It was then, filled with reverence and awe, that we began to speak of the mystery of being alive in this place amidst the stars. Sitting there, watching sparks float upward and disappear against the milky, jeweled heavens, we considered what it would be like to create our lives as an art form—not just to live casually, half-consciously, doing what everyone else does until we all die, but to dedicate ourselves to compassionate service, to a celebration of being alive, and to an unceasing battle against negativity.

Your life is something you *create*, moment by moment. You are ultimately responsible for where you are, who you're with, and what you're doing. Like a painting, a sculpture, or a pottery bowl, you can create something fine and useful with your life, or you can throw it away. You have the power to make a life of great quality, or to ruin it. Most of us, fearing failure and not fully aware of our mortality, surrender all too soon to a second-rate (at best) way of life.

The concept of good form is familiar to every athlete. Depending upon your sport, it might refer to proper line, correct execution of a skill, or efficiency of movement. In whole-body training, good form also applies equally to the mind and the emotins.

Good physical form is the most efficient (and therefore the most aesthetic) way of blending with, and using, the natural laws. This involves

• Proper alignment with gravity, in stillness and motion, flowing with all forces of nature.

- No unnecessary tension; easy does it.
- Unified musculature, letting the left hand know what the right hand is doing.
- Awareness and use of energies; sensing the lines of force.
- Coordinated response and timing, being in the right place at the right time.

You can apply the principle of good physical form to your game, as well as all ordinary movements during the day.

Good mental form is the releasing of thoughts as they arise, directing your attention to your movements. This means dropping all self-criticism, fear, anger, idle fantasy, and concern.

Good emotional form is breathing consciously, with feeling; it's the discipline of *feeling* happy, without cause or reason. *Happiness is the ultimate emotional discipline.*

In sport, the athlete works to avoid form breaks. In life, the natural athlete applies himself with equal intensity to maintain good form—through the body, mind, and emotions.

There are always good reasons to justify form breaks. If your physical form is poor, the reason may be weak muscles or lack of awareness. If your emotional form is poor, if you're feeling and acting unhappy, perhaps it's because a jumbo jet just made an unscheduled landing on your best friend. That's a very good reason to feel tense. Mental form breaks—distractions, divided attention—also have reasons. Yet, whatever the reasons, you are still left with a fundamental choice in every moment: You can let the form break remain (and justify it), or you can correct it.

It is your life; create what you will. You always have a choice. If you apply the lessons of nature, and strive to maintain whole-body good form in daily life and athletics, your discipline will transform you.

11 THE ATHLETE'S MEDITATION

The nature of spiritual training

Spiritual training is whole-body training. When your movement, emotional, and intellectual functions are in complete harmony, the world literally changes for you. It's not that a table or chair becomes something else, it's just that life becomes simultaneously less complicated and more interesting. All the problems and complexities of your life, which seem to be imposed upon you by circumstance, are nothing more than symptoms of internal contradiction—disharmony among body, mind, and emotions.

The unified state frees your attention, so that for the first time, you become aware of subtle mechanisms and intuitions you had rarely seen before. There are moments you even feel psychic; moments you experience such total empathy with someone that you feel you can read his thoughts.

More today than ever, in popular literature on sport and psychology, athletes report extraordinary experiences while immersed in the Moment of Truth. Their experiences range from a feeling of extranormal abilities, to moments of absolute ecstasy, beyond words. Some athletes have reported a sense that time slows almost to a standstill; others have emotionally described being lost in a dance of time, so that hours seemed like minutes. Many of us have felt a dazzling sensory clarity during the heat of competition, when we felt "really alive."

All these experiences point to the *meditative demand* of sport. Every athlete literally must meditate on every move he makes, giving total attention to his relations with the environment—and no attention to internal noise. The athlete in the Moment of Truth is undivided. Without knowing it, he has, like the Indian yogi, been practicing meditation.

Several years ago, when I observed Japanese Olympic ski jumpers warming up with t'ai chi and saw aikido masters teaching golf clinics, it became apparent that the golden threads of East-West movement forms were weaving a new fabric for the world's enjoyment. I began to approach my coaching with an Eastern as well as Western flavor, and thereby gained a reputation (back then) as a "little bit eccentric." I was always amused when another coach would ask me incredulously, "Is it true that you have your gymnasts *meditate* before every competition?" "Of course not," I'd reply. "We meditate *during* the competition."

The athlete's satori

Satori is a word from the Japanese Zen tradition which describes the natural harmony of body, mind, and emotions.

When the *mind*, free of internal distractions, is pure attention to the present moment.

• When the *emotions*, free of obstructing tension, manifest as pure motivational energy.

• When the *body*, fully relaxed and vitalized, is sensitive and open to life.

When the three centers are in this simultaneous relationship, something clicks; that's *satori*. It represents a state which the athlete, artist, musician, and every performing artist flashes in and out of on many occasions. You can, in fact, experience it right now.

▷ **INSTANT SATORI**

Take your keys, a piece of fruit, or any handy object, and go outside. Throw the object up into the air. Staying relaxed and easy, catch it. Be sure to catch it. Then come back inside, and continue reading.

Consider the moment that object was in the air. You weren't thinking of what you'd have for dinner or what you did yesterday. You weren't thinking of anything else, either. You may have been attending to thoughts before you threw it or after you caught it, but during the throw, you were pure attention, reaching out, waiting for the object's descent. In that same moment, your emotions were open, and your body was alert and vitalized. That was a moment of satori.

Satori feels good. It's the state that athletes describe in glowing metaphors, the state Zen archers shoot for. It's the natural state of the natural athlete. Satori is dynamic meditation; it's the "reason" we enjoy sports.

Athletes and artists of every kind are *satori seekers*, because that state represents a momentary "vacation," free of problems or complications, free of past or future. We may become attached to all manner of out-of-the-ordinary experiences, but they are only variations of unity. Satori is the hidden goal behind all our aspirations. Satori is the core of the moving experience. It's the clue which sends us onward, the great pathway; it's a preview of spiritual life.

As an infant, you were once the natural athlete. And so you can be again. You don't have to reach the Olympian heights to be a natural athlete; you don't even have to be an athlete. Straining muscles and sweat are not a prerequisite. All you have to do is find a way, a means to carry you on your journey. Do it with all your mind and feeling and vitality; do it with all your spirit. Approach training and daily life in the same way. Do not be content to stumble passively upon the spiritual experience for flashing seconds, but dedicate your training toward conscious development of the three centers. This is the culmination of your journey. As your mind becomes disciplined and free, your heart will open, your body will come alive.

Closer and closer you come to the top of the mountain. Almost without noticing it, you begin to step to the rhythms of nature, and you bathe in satori. As you round the last bend in the path and see the peak before you, you notice someone standing there, smiling at you with bright, clear eyes. It is the Master of Daily Life. You approach closer—you walk right up to him, and reach out to touch him, filled with gratitude. Suddenly, he disappears, and in that moment, you realize that the Master is . . . you.

Epilogue

The university remains the domain of the intellect. The temple is the domain of the heart. The gymnasium is the arena of vitality. You have the university, the temple, and the gymnasium within you. The journey before you—in becoming a natural athlete—is to rebuild and reconnect these centers so they work as one. Athletes are inclined to spend more time building the gymnasium. Others are more drawn to fixing up the temple or the university. Each must be given its equal share. The reward is commensurate with the effort.

What perhaps began as a quest for athletic improvement is now, I hope, imbued with greater scope and promise than you might have anticipated. Athletics can be, truly, the Game of Life.

We humans stand at the last frontier—the inward journey. The total athlete discovers the laws of the universe within his own body. As I worked on this book late at night or in the wee hours of morning, images of natural order, balance, nonresistance, satori, blending, energy flow, the Moment of Truth all whirled and danced, like glowing spirits, weaving a pattern of new possibilities.

You can bring such possibilities into life. I want to wish you the most enjoyable training . . . as mindless as a tree, as light as a cloud, fast as a hummingbird's wing, merry as a star's twinkle . . . and bright as the morning sun.

The following chart contains the fundamental qualities of physical, emotional, and mental talent which apply to athletics—and also contribute toward a healthful, functional, and positive approach to daily life.

The chart may be used as a tool for realistic self-observation, as a report card (filled out by a teacher or coach), or as a visible predictor of whole-body talent.

The graph, which will probably look something like

clearly shows strong and weak areas. As you've learned, once weak areas are clearly seen, a strong psychological impulse is put into action.

You can use this chart as a basis for an athletic diary, so you can begin to learn about yourself through training. Most people experience inertia (in the guise of lack of interest in filling out such a chart) when they first look at the graph. Nevertheless, if you make use of it even occasionally, it will serve you.

A GUIDE FOR PREDICTING PSYCHOPHYSICAL TALENT

Rate each area below from 1 (very weak) to 10 (ideal). Connect the dots to form a graph of whole-body talent. Repeat each month to chart improvements. Pay special attention to weak areas; a horizontal line (indicating no weaknesses) is ideal. This graph may appear complex, but is actually a simple and useful method of self-observation and whole-body development.

Body

	A	B	C	D	E
10	—	—	—	—	—
9	—	—	—	—	—
8	—	—	—	—	—
7	—	—	—	—	—
6	—	—	—	—	—
5	—	—	—	—	—
4	—	—	—	—	—
3	—	—	—	—	—
2	—	—	—	—	—
1	—	—	—	—	—

A. Suppleness
B. Strength and control
C. Relaxed movement; no tension
D. Sensitivity: timing, rhythm, etc.
E. Stamina; endurance

Emotions

	A	B	C	D	E
10	—	—	—	—	—
9	—	—	—	—	—
8	—	—	—	—	—
7	—	—	—	—	—
6	—	—	—	—	—
5	—	—	—	—	—
4	—	—	—	—	—
3	—	—	—	—	—
2	—	—	—	—	—
1	—	—	—	—	—

A. Nondramatization
B. Positive spirit
C. Cooperative, helping attitudes
D. Using talk wisely
E. Enjoying your present level

Mind

	A	B	C	D	E
10	—	—	—	—	—
9	—	—	—	—	—
8	—	—	—	—	—
7	—	—	—	—	—
6	—	—	—	—	—
5	—	—	—	—	—
4	—	—	—	—	—
3	—	—	—	—	—
2	—	—	—	—	—
1	—	—	—	—	—

A. Intelligent use of time
B. Balanced training for health
C. Turning knowledge to action
D. Realistic goals; proper effort
E. Attention to the present

Comments: